# MARY BERRY

# COOK NOW EAT LATER

# MARY BERRY
# COOK NOW
# EAT LATER
## RECIPES THAT MAKE
## YOUR LIFE EASIER

headline

Mary Berry is well known as the author of more than seventy cookery books with total sales of over 5 million. She has presented a number of television series and is currently a judge on *The Great British Bake Off*. She contributes to radio programmes and cookery magazines, and is loved for her practical and unfussy approach. She gives many demonstrations around the country but when she is at home, she loves to be with her family and tending her garden – her other great passion.

Copyright © 2014 Mary Berry

Photographs © 2014 Martin Poole

The right of Mary Berry to be identified as the Author of the Work has been asserted by her in accordance with the Copyright, Designs and Patents Act 1988.

This edition first published in 2014 by HEADLINE BOOK PUBLISHING

**Cook Now Eat Later** was first published in 2002

Apart from any use permitted under UK copyright law, this publication may only be reproduced, stored, or transmitted, in any form, or by any means, with prior permission in writing of the publishers or, in the case of reprographic production, in accordance with the terms of licence issued by the Copyright Licensing Agency.

Every effort has been made to fulfil requirements with regard to reproducing copyright material. The author and publisher will be glad to rectify any omissions at the earliest opportunity.

Cataloguing in Publication Data is available from the British Library

ISBN 9781472214737

Photographs by Martin Poole
Edited by Jo Roberts-Miller
Designed by Smith & Gilmour
Food Stylist Kim Morphew
Assistant Food Stylist Poppy Campbell
Prop Stylist Lydia Brun
Printed and bound in China by C&C offset Prining Co., Ltd

Headline's policy is to use papers that are natural, renewable and recyclable products and made from wood grown in sustainable forests. The logging and manufacturing processes are expected to conform to the environmental regulations of the country of origin.

HEADLINE BOOK PUBLISHING
An Hachette UK Company
Carmelite House
50 Victoria Embankment
London EC4Y 0DZ

www.headline.co.uk
www.hachette.com

# CONTENTS

This book is all about being organised. It's about preparing and cooking ahead, whether you are feeding the family casually in the kitchen or friends more formally in the dining room. We all love entertaining, but sometimes the reality of the many separate parts involved in a meal can seem daunting. How long will the pudding take to set? When can I prepare the vegetables? Will the potatoes be ready at the same time as the meat? Will the whole house smell of fish when I sear the sea bass skin? When can I talk to my friends if I'm stuck in the kitchen? Panic can set in, but that's where I will come to your rescue.

In a book such as this, where the concept is 'cook now, eat later', it would be easy to give you recipes that could all be cooked completely in advance and that merely needed reheating. Easy, yes, but a bit boring. What I have done is gather together my very latest, up-to-the-minute recipes, many of which, I will happily admit, need some last-minute attention. But various stages of them can be prepared and/or cooked in advance, which means that on the day itself, you will have much less to do, and will not feel too much immediate pressure. The recipes themselves are divided into easy-to-follow numbered steps, and that's essentially what I want to do here: help you to be one step ahead of the game.

Being organised, so far as food and entertaining are concerned, is not just to do with the actual cooking. For instance, if you order the fish or meat you want well in advance from fishmonger, butcher or supermarket, that's one aspect of the meal taken care of. We all think freshly prepared is best, but many vegetables can be peeled, trimmed and cut at least the day before, which means one less chore on the day. And don't ever be ashamed of cutting corners to enable you to be organised and ahead. Buy ready-prepared vegetables or salad leaves in packets if you think you won't have time: they're more expensive, but your peace of mind might be more important than cost. Even counting out the napkins, and checking on candles and cutlery a couple of days in advance, puts you a step or so ahead.

But the majority of the information here does actually concern some degree of cooking, and when you are doing this in advance, there are certain stages which must be followed. The refrigerator is intimately involved in this, and the 'rules' concerning cooling and chilling are particularly important. Make sure your fridge is working properly. The ideal temperature for the short-term storage of perishable foods is just above freezing point. Individual makes of fridges vary, but the temperature range should be between 1°C and 7°C (34°–44°F).

# Preparing and Cooking Ahead

I won't detail every single way in which you can prepare and cook ahead, but just give you a few general ideas.

Firstly preparation, which does not require cooking. Many non-cooked cold starters and desserts can be completely prepared ahead and stored in the fridge to set and/or chill. Meats, fish and vegetables can be marinated overnight in the fridge, ready for cooking the next day. Many vegetables can be prepared in advance and kept raw in the fridge. Savoury butters – handy for so many uses – last well in the fridge, and some uncooked stuffings can be assembled with meats or fish and carefully chilled until it's time to cook. Raw pastry, bought or home-made, positively benefits from being kept in the fridge, after rolling and cutting into the desired shapes.

Everything must be carefully covered to prevent smells permeating where they shouldn't or surfaces drying. Clingfilm and foil are invaluable tools for those who want to get ahead. Some foods need to breathe when stored, like cheese, which is best wrapped in greaseproof or wax paper.

Cooking ahead lies at the heart of the book. Many dishes require part-cooking a day or hours before, and then finishing off at the last minute. Some fish, for instance, can be seared briefly to brown the day before, then chilled and baked or grilled for a few minutes before serving. The same can apply to some poultry and game dishes, especially prime cuts such as breasts. Many stew-type dishes and soups can be completely

cooked ahead and kept in the fridge for a couple of days – and most of these can be frozen (see overleaf). Root vegetables can be char-grilled ahead then blasted with heat at the last minute.

In general, try to slightly *under*cook things if cooking completely ahead. You will have to reheat until piping hot and you don't want things to overcook and disintegrate. Even if the main ingredient in a meal cannot be cooked in advance – like roast lamb, for instance – you can pre- or part-cook its accompaniments.

Suggested cooking times and cooking techniques are given for the Aga alongside each recipe. When the top of the oven is used, obviously cooking on the Aga hotplates is very similar and so I haven't gone into too much detail there. But occasionally, instead of cooking on the Simmering Plate and losing heat by keeping the lid up for a long time, you can cover and cook something like onions in the Simmering Oven. Bring a sauce, stew or casserole to the boil on the Boiling Plate then cover, transfer to the Simmering Oven and cook until tender. This means that, although they take longer to cook, they will not boil over, they don't need to be watched, and they will be beautifully tender. And, most importantly, the Aga will not lose too much heat through the open lids.

# Cooling and Chilling

These are vital elements of preparing and cooking ahead. When you have partially or completely cooked something, you want it to cool as quickly as possible before chilling. The first thing to do is simple: take off the lid! One option with a casserole-type dish is to decant it from its hot cooking pot into two smaller, cold dishes, or a shallow roasting tray. This means that more surface area is exposed to cool air, but also means extra washing-up, so I'm not too keen. And I don't think you need to use cold water baths or ice. A cool ambient temperature, such as a larder or pantry, should be sufficient.

Once a dish is cool, it must then be covered with a lid, clingfilm or foil, and stored in the fridge for the recommended time. And if you haven't room enough in your own fridge, ask your friends and neighbours to lend theirs. It's the least they can do if they're coming to eat your delicious food!

Never add a garnish to a cooked dish before chilling and/or freezing. Do so when it is reheated, immediately before serving.

ORANGE CURD ICE CREAM

# Freezing and Thawing

The freezer can be used very creatively when you are planning, preparing and cooking ahead. Even if you just use it to freeze basics such as butter or bread, you can be one step ahead in that you don't have to rush to the shops at the last minute. And blanched home-grown green vegetables can be happily frozen. If you like to cook things fresh at the last moment, there are a number of dishes here that can be prepared – the Chilean Chicken on page 89, for example – and frozen raw. Sauces, stocks and soups can be made and frozen well in advance, as can dishes in sauces, such as casseroles or curries. Baked goods can also be frozen very successfully – a huge advantage when someone phones up to invite themselves to tea!

When freezing, always clearly label the dish with a permanent marker pen – the date, the amount it serves and what it is. There is nothing more annoying than finding food in the freezer you have no idea about! You could also add any useful comment you have room for on the label, such as 'specially good', or 'serve with mash' etc. Freeze soup in meal-sized containers – this avoids having to defrost the whole lot for one person. (Don't add the cream to a soup if you are freezing it: do that when you are reheating.) Freeze stock in old cream or yoghurt pots – 300–600ml (½–1 pint) plastic pots – then when the recipe states 600ml (1 pint) it is easy to take out just the required amount from the freezer.

When making a complete dish – lasagne or moussaka, say – freeze raw in the dish you are going to cook it in. If you need the dish while it is in the freezer, thaw it for about an hour, loosen the edges, turn out in one solid lump and put in a bag back in the freezer. The dish can then be used and the frozen lasagne can be put back into the dish when it is free again.

Always thaw in the fridge overnight before cooking, and do not cook something in a dish straight from the freezer or the heat of the oven is likely to crack the dish. Do remember, though, that some things are just not suitable for the freezer. In each of the recipes throughout the book, I give detailed timing instructions, or warn you against.

# Reheating and Refreshing

When a dish is taken straight from the fridge, whether it is fully cooked or partially cooked, it will be cold, and therefore could take slightly longer to cook to piping hot – the desired temperature. Use your judgement and, where useful, I have mentioned this in the recipe notes. (Incidentally, a thick dish will need its cooking time extended as well.)

If taking an ovenproof porcelain dish straight from the fridge, remember to let it come to room temperature for a little while before cooking, so that the dish doesn't crack from the shock in the oven.

'Refreshing' is the term used for bringing back to life baked goods in general after they have been chilled or defrosted. Breads always taste better when they are warm, but some muffins and scones can taste like new when reheated. It must not be an extreme heat – you don't want to make many things crisp and dry – but just enough to warm the food through thoroughly.

I've suggested a few pasta recipes here and, perhaps surprisingly, the pasta can be cooked up to 6 hours in advance. I always use dried pasta when I plan to do this. What you do is cook the pasta in plenty of boiling salted water until al dente, still with a slight bite in the centre. Refresh in plenty of cold running water. Leave the cold pasta in the colander, and cover with clingfilm. To reheat, either tip the pasta into the hot sauce if the pasta has a sauce with it, or plunge into boiling salted water for a few moments, stirring until the pasta is piping hot. Drain and serve at once.

A good number of people these days prefer to eat in the kitchen with friends rather than give more formal dinner parties. And of course, when people are milling around you in the kitchen – chatting, laughing, perhaps even trying to help (or interfering!) – you want to be as well organised and as well ahead as possible. You don't want your knife technique to come under criticism, or any unwashed pots to be too much in evidence.

I have aimed for as many recipes as possible to be prepared and cooked at least a day before, and then reheated, which allows you to mingle happily with your guests, share a drink with them, and enjoy the evening without any hassle in the kitchen.

Those, then, are the 'rules'! Now I hope you will enjoy cooking these recipes as much as we have enjoyed testing them. Remember always that cooking should be fun. If you follow my advice about preparing and cooking ahead, I think you will recognise that that is true. Cooking *is* a true pleasure (so long as you are well organised!) and you will be able to relax and enjoy eating with your friends and family.

COOK NOW, EAT LATER

✦

# Starters
# and Nibbles

CHAPTER ONE

The starter is the first thing your guests will see and sample, so it must look and taste good. I like to arrange my cold starters on the table ready for when we go into the kitchen or dining room. I think it looks so welcoming – and so organised! This is practical as well, because if the starters have been in the fridge, they always need a little time at room temperature: if food is too cold, you can't taste anything. Cold starters are commonly considered to be the most useful for the cook. They need very little last-minute attention, certainly in the way of cooking, and if the dessert is cold as well, it allows you to spend more time and energy on the main course (usually the high point of any meal) and, most important of all, more time with your guests.

However, hot starters should never be ignored, because if you are organised and prepare the basics well in advance, a final quick heat through in the oven or under the grill – which is all most of them need – is easy. And a hot starter, particularly on a cold winter's day, is always welcome. Soups are perhaps the easiest of the lot, as most can be made at least 1 month in advance and frozen. All you need to do is remember to defrost them overnight, or, at a pinch, melt the frozen block gently in a saucepan. (And I think hot plates for soup are vital: warm soup is *not* the same as hot soup.)

Preparing what I call 'bits and bobs' for drinks parties is generally considered to be very labour-intensive. And so it is: everything is smaller, so shaping, cutting and putting toppings and garnishes on bases is much more intricate and detailed. All the recipes here can be prepared in advance, though, so the bulk of the work is out of the way. All you will have to do on the day is make things look pretty on platters. Dips are very useful, and the two here can be made in advance, and used with crudités or spread on crostini or pitta breads. The crostini themselves are a huge life-saver: store them in the freezer in plastic boxes with kitchen paper in between the layers. They're immediately to hand, take no time to defrost, and are great for any topping.

Most of the recipes here are simple to make, though some might seem a little more complicated. But as the method is divided up into separate stages, you should never find it too much of a chore. Soufflés, for instance, are said to be the bane of most cooks' lives, but mine can be cooked up to 2 days in advance (actually they can even be frozen), and then given a quick blast in a hot oven to puff them up. And don't forget to serve hot bread or rolls with the first course. You can buy some lovely breads now in bakeries and supermarkets, and warming them through makes most taste even better. If you make the rolls on page 238, freeze them in quantities for the number of guests you expect, then simply defrost and heat.

V

# Mustard and Parmesan Cheese Straws

Cheese straws that aren't too fiddly! The mustard
gives a lovely dark colour to the straws, too.

1 × 375g (13 oz) packet ready-
  rolled all-butter puff pastry,
  approx. 35.5 × 23cm
  (14 × 9 in)
2–3 tablespoons
  Dijon mustard

50g (2 oz) Parmesan or
  Parmesan-style hard
  cheese, grated
salt and freshly ground
  black pepper
1 large egg, beaten

Preheat the oven to 220°C/Fan 200°C/Gas 7. Lightly
grease 2 baking trays or line the trays with non-stick
baking paper.

**1** Unroll the pastry on a floured work surface and
spread the mustard over the top. Sprinkle evenly
with the Parmesan, salt and pepper. Cover with
clingfilm and, using a rolling pin, roll the cheese
into the pastry for a few minutes. Remove
the clingfilm.

**2** Divide the pastry in 4 widthways and cut each
section into 10 strips about 1cm (½ in) thick
for each straw. Twist each straw and place on
the prepared baking trays. For extra long cheese
straws, cut the pastry in half widthways and divide
each section into 8 strips, about 2.5cm (1 in) thick.

**3** Glaze with the beaten egg and bake in the
preheated oven for about 8–10 minutes (12 minutes
for the long straws). Check the short straws after
5 minutes, the long after 8, to make sure they are
not getting too brown. When the pastry is cooked
through and golden brown, remove from the baking
sheet and cool on a cooling rack.

**COOK NOW EAT LATER**

**TO PREPARE AHEAD**
These can be made,
cooked, cooled and
kept in the larder
for 2–3 days. When
storing, place between
kitchen paper in a
sealed container –
this will stop them
from becoming soggy.
Refresh in an oven
preheated to 200°C/Fan
180°C/Gas 6 for a few
minutes to regain their
crispness before serving.

**TO FREEZE**
Cook, cool and freeze
for up to 2 months.
Thaw for about
15 minutes at room
temperature. Refresh
in the oven as above.

**TO COOK IN THE AGA**
Bake on the floor of
the Roasting Oven
for about 8 minutes,
checking after 4. If
the straws are getting
too brown, slide the
cold sheet on to the
second set of runners.

# Summer Pea, Spring Onion and Mint Soup

**V** · **SERVES 6**

A perfect soup using fresh flavours for summer days.

**COOK NOW EAT LATER**

**TO PREPARE AHEAD**
Can be made up
to 2 days ahead
and reheated to serve.

**TO FREEZE**
Freezes well puréed.

**TO COOK IN THE AGA**
Make on the Boiling
Plate.

1 tablespoon olive oil
a knob of butter
1 shallot, finely chopped
1 small potato, peeled and
diced (approx 150g/5 oz
peeled weight)
8 fat spring onions, trimmed
and chopped (reserve one
for garnish)

1.1 litres (2 pints)
vegetable stock
2 tablespoons fresh mint
leaves (reserve a few
tiny leaves to garnish)
salt and freshly ground
black pepper
900g (2 lb) frozen
petits pois

**1** Heat a deep pan over a high heat and then add the oil
and butter. Once melted add the shallot, potato and
spring onions. Fry for 5 minutes, stirring.

**2** Add the stock and mint leaves and season with salt
and pepper. Bring to the boil, cover and simmer for
about 15 minutes.

**3** Add the frozen peas, bring back to the boil and boil
for 15 minutes, or until the potato and peas are tender.

**4** Meanwhile, cut the reserved spring onion into very thin
strips (about 5 cm/2 in long) and put into a bowl of very
cold water. Set aside for them to curl and use as garnish.

**5** Cool the soup for a few moments, then whiz in a food
processor or with a blender until smooth. If it is a little
thick, add some more water.

**6** Pour back in the pan, bring back to the boil, and check
the seasoning. Serve in warm soup bowls, garnished
with a few small mint leaves and curls of spring onion.

# Winter Vegetable Soup

**V** · SERVES 6

This is a lovely home-made soup, using all vegetables in season, and has been our favourite soup this winter. It is delicious as a first course when there's not much to follow, or for lunch on a cold winter's day. If you are in a hurry, use a food processor to chop the vegetables, but be sure to leave them quite chunky.

COOK NOW
EAT LATER

## TO PREPARE AHEAD
Cool the soup after step 3, cover and store in the fridge for up to 3 days. Bring to the boil and scatter parsley on top to serve.

## TO FREEZE
Cool the soup after step 3 and pour into a freezer container, cover and freeze for up to 1 month. Thaw at room temperature for about 8 hours, or overnight in the fridge.

## TO COOK IN THE AGA
At step 1, cook the vegetables covered in the Simmering Oven for about 10 minutes to soften. Return the pan to the Simmering Oven at step 3, cover and cook for about 15–30 minutes until the vegetables are tender.

50g (2 oz) butter
2 small red onions, finely chopped
2 leeks, finely chopped
3 celery sticks, finely sliced
2 large garlic cloves, crushed
4 level tablespoons plain flour
500ml (18 fl oz) tomato passata
2 large potatoes, peeled and finely diced
1 × 400g can chopped tomatoes
1–2 level tablespoons caster sugar
2 tablespoons tomato purée
1.1 litres (2 pints) chicken or vegetable stock
salt and freshly ground black pepper
lots of chopped fresh parsley

**1** Melt the butter in a large saucepan and add the onions, leeks, celery and garlic. Stir over a high heat for a few minutes, then lower the heat, cover the pan and cook gently for about 10 minutes to soften.

**2** Whisk the flour with a quarter of the passata in a bowl until well blended and smooth. Add the remaining passata.

**3** Add the potatoes, tomatoes, sugar and tomato purée to the pan. Blend in the passata and the stock, stir and allow to thicken. Bring to the boil and season. Cover and cook over a gentle heat for about 20–30 minutes or until the vegetables are tender.

**4** Check seasoning and serve hot, scattered with plenty of parsley.

# The Very Best Porcini Mushroom Soup

Mushroom soup is a classic but there are very few tasty ones with intense flavour, which is why we use dried porcini. Older mushrooms will give the soup a better colour and flavour, and they are sometimes sold off more cheaply. You will find it easier to strain off the mushroom and onion into a sieve and just process the vegetables, adding a little of the liquid rather than lots of batches. Return to the pan with the strained liquid.

20–25g (¾–1 oz) dried porcini (cep) mushrooms
150ml (¼ pint) water
40g (1½ oz) butter
2 large Spanish onions, finely chopped
2 large garlic cloves, crushed
700g (1½ lb) open mushrooms, roughly sliced
75g (3 oz) plain flour
75ml (⅛ pint) white wine

1.7 litres (3 pints) good chicken, turkey or vegetable stock
salt and freshly ground black pepper
2 tablespoons dark soy sauce
1 teaspoon lemon juice
3 tablespoons double cream
3 tablespoons sherry (optional)
lots of chopped fresh parsley

**COOK NOW EAT LATER**

### TO PREPARE AHEAD
Cool the soup after step 5, transfer to a container and keep in the fridge for up to 3 days. Reheat until piping hot, then add the cream and parsley and serve.

### TO FREEZE
Cool the soup after step 5 and pour into a freezer container, cover and freeze for up to 1 month. Thaw at room temperature for about 8 hours, or overnight in the fridge. Or, if you are in a hurry, put the frozen block of soup in a pan over a low heat, stirring!

**1** Soak the porcini mushrooms for 30 minutes in the water.

**2** Melt the butter in a deep saucepan, add the onions and fry on a high heat for a few minutes, without colouring. Lower the heat, cover the pan and cook gently for about 10 minutes until the onion is tender. Add the garlic and open mushrooms and fry over a high heat, stirring all the time, for a further 2–3 minutes.

**3** Measure the flour, wine and a small amount of cold stock into a bowl and whisk until smooth.

*Recipe continued overleaf*

COOK NOW EAT LATER

## TO COOK IN THE AGA

Cook the onion covered in a pan in the Simmering Oven for about 20 minutes in step 2, and 15–20 minutes covered in the Simmering Oven, in step 4.

## TIP

Cep and porcini mushrooms are the same – 'cep' or 'cepe' is French in origin and 'porcini' is Italian. They can be found fresh but are mostly available dried. They add intense flavour to soups and stews, and are usually soaked for about 20–30 minutes in warm water before cooking. Add the soaking liquid, too, as this has a wonderfully intense flavour (strain it well to get rid of any grit).

*Recipe continued*

**4** Remove the pan from the heat and slowly stir in the flour mixture and the rest of the stock, stirring until well blended and smooth. Bring to the boil for a couple of minutes until thickened, then add the porcini mushrooms and their carefully strained soaking liquid. Season with salt, pepper, soy sauce and lemon juice. Cover and simmer gently for 15–20 minutes.

**5** Allow to cool slightly (until safe enough to handle). Transfer to a food processor and blend until smooth. The soup will not be completely smooth but will still have some texture from the mushrooms.

**6** Check the seasoning and stir in the cream and sherry (if using). Garnish generously with chopped parsley and serve with some warm crusty bread.

COOK NOW 26 EAT LATER
STARTERS AND NIBBLES

# Peppadew and Chèvre Crostini

Peppadew peppers can be bought in jars in good supermarkets
as mild or hot peppers. We use mild.

**COOK NOW
EAT LATER**

### TO PREPARE AHEAD

Prepare to step 5
up to 8 hours ahead.
Cover with clingfilm
and keep in the fridge
until ready to cook.
Flash under a hot
grill for 5 minutes
when guests arrive.

### TO FREEZE

The crostini bases
can be made up to
2 months ahead and
frozen. Leave at room
temperature until
defrosted.

### TO COOK IN THE AGA

Bake the bread on
a solid baking sheet
on the floor of the
Roasting Oven for
about 5–6 minutes
until pale golden,
turning halfway
through. At step 6,
heat the crostini
on the second set
of runners in the
Roasting Oven for
about 5 minutes until
warm right through.

about 2 tablespoons olive oil
1 garlic clove, crushed
a thin French stick/baguette
150g (5 oz) goat's cheese,
  in a roll
a little double cream
1 × 375g jar peppadew
  peppers
fresh basil leaves
  to garnish

Preheat the grill to its highest setting.

**1** Mix together the oil and garlic in a small
ramekin or bowl.

**2** Thinly slice the baguette and brush both sides
with the garlic-flavoured olive oil. Place the bread
on a small baking sheet which will fit under the
grill, or line the grill pan with foil.

**3** To cook the crostini, toast under the preheated
grill for about 2–3 minutes each side until pale
golden brown and crisp. Watch them carefully.
Cool on a wire rack.

**4** Mash the goat's cheese (use the rind as well)
with a little cream. Spread on to the cold crostini,
keeping a little back.

**5** Drain and dry about 15 peppers, coarsely chop
and arrange on the cheese. Dot the peppers with
an additional piece of cheese.

**6** Heat the crostini for about 5 minutes under the
preheated hot grill. Garnish each crostini with
a basil leaf and serve.

# Tiny New Potatoes
## with Dill Herrings

An unusual canapé to go with drinks. Buy the smallest new potatoes you can buy.
Dill herrings come in a jar (found in the chilled section of any good supermarket
with pâtés and smoked salmon) and are very versatile.

10 very small new potatoes,
   skin on
1 × 275g jar herrings
   in dill marinade

3 tablespoons crème fraîche
a few sprigs of fresh dill

**TO PREPARE AHEAD**
These can be
completely made up
to 12 hours ahead,
and kept in the fridge.

**TO FREEZE**
Not suitable.

**1** Cook the potatoes in boiling salted water until tender,
about 8–10 minutes. Drain, refresh in cold water (to stop
the cooking), leave to cool and dry.

**2** Slice the potatoes in half lengthways. Slice a very thin
layer from the rounded end of each potato half (opposite
the sliced side), so they will sit flat on a plate.

**3** Drain the herrings from the marinade and slice into 1cm
(½ in) pieces (or pieces about half the size of the potato).
Spoon a tiny blob of crème fraîche on top of each potato
and place a piece of herring on top, with a sprig of dill
to garnish.

# Onion, Apple and Stilton Little Quiches

**v** SERVES 8

A delicious variation on an old favourite of ours, the apple and sage giving a wonderfully unusual flavour. Make these in two 4-portion Yorkshire pudding tins, to make 8 individual tarts. This pastry is really cheesy and delicious, and is well worth making if you have time. If time is short, use bought shortcrust pastry instead of home-made.

## Herb and Cheese Pastry

175g (6 oz) plain flour
½ teaspoon salt
1 teaspoon mustard powder
75g (3 oz) butter, cut into small pieces
1 teaspoon chopped fresh sage
50g (2 oz) Parmesan or Parmesan-style hard cheese, freshly grated
1 large egg, beaten

## Filling

1 tablespoon olive oil
1 large Spanish onion, thinly sliced
100g (4 oz) cooking apple, peeled and coarsely grated
½ teaspoon sugar
100g (4 oz) Stilton cheese, grated
2 large eggs
scant 200ml (⅓ pint) double cream
salt and freshly ground black pepper
1 teaspoon coarsely chopped fresh sage

COOK NOW
EAT LATER

**TO PREPARE AHEAD**
Make the pastry up to 1 day ahead and line the tins. Cook the apple and onion, cool and divide between the tarts, add the Stilton, cover and keep in the fridge up to 8 hours ahead. Pour in the cream and egg mixture and sprinkle with the sage just before cooking. The tartlets can also be cooked completely ahead and reheated in an oven preheated to 200°C/Fan 180°C/Gas 6 for about 10 minutes. Keep an eye on them.

**TO FREEZE**
The cooked tarts freeze well. Cool, wrap, and freeze for up to 3 months. Thaw for about 4 hours at room temperature and reheat to serve as above.

**1** First make the pastry. Measure the flour, salt, mustard, butter and sage into the food processor or a bowl, and process or rub until the mixture resembles fine breadcrumbs. Add the Parmesan and the beaten egg and mix again for just as long as it takes for the ingredients to come together. Chill for 30 minutes wrapped in clingfilm.

*Recipe continued overleaf*

*Recipe continued*

## TO COOK IN THE AGA

Cook the filling as in step 2, covered, in the Simmering Oven, for about 15–20 minutes. Bake the assembled tarts on the grid shelf on the floor of the Roasting Oven for 15–20 minutes, turning around halfway through the cooking time, until set and pale golden. If the pastry is not brown underneath put the tins directly on the floor of the oven for a few minutes.

**2** For the filling, heat the oil in a pan and cook the onion over a high heat for a few minutes. Cover and cook over a low heat until soft, about 10–15 minutes. Return to a high heat, add the apple and fry for a further 5 minutes, stirring all the time. Add the sugar, and cook for a few minutes without the lid to evaporate any liquid from the onion. Cool.

**3** Roll the pastry thinly on a lightly floured work surface. Using an 11.5cm (4 ¾ in) cutter, cut out 8 discs. Use these to line 2 × 4-hole Yorkshire pudding trays. Chill if time allows.

Preheat the oven to 220°C/Fan 200°C/Gas 7. Put 2 baking sheets into the oven to heat.

**4** Divide the cold onion and apple between the tartlet cases and top with the Stilton.

**5** Beat the eggs and add the cream and seasoning. Carefully pour the egg and cream mixture into the tartlets, then sprinkle evenly with sage.

**6** Put the Yorkshire pudding tins on top of the preheated baking sheets and bake in the oven for about 15–20 minutes until the tarts are set and pale golden.

# Twice-baked Tomato and Feta Soufflés

SERVES 6

Everyone loves a hot first course, so one that can be made ahead and reheated at the last minute is a real winner. This also makes a delicious lunch dish, served with crusty bread and a mixed leaf salad. Who said making a soufflé was difficult? Sun-blushed tomatoes are half-dried tomatoes which are less chewy than the usual sun-dried variety, though sun-dried can be used if you are unable to find sun-blushed. Passata is sieved tomatoes and can be bought in cartons or bottles. If only using half the bottle, freeze the remainder, but use within 2 months. Like tomato purée, it goes off quickly in the fridge.

**COOK NOW EAT LATER**

## TO PREPARE AHEAD

Up to 48 hours ahead, turn the cooked soufflés out on to the buttered and Parmesan-sprinkled dish. Don't sprinkle with the remaining Parmesan or pour in the passata yet. Cover with foil and keep in the fridge. Continue as from step 5.

## TO FREEZE

Freeze the wrapped, cooked soufflés for up to 1 month. Thaw at room temperature for about 6 hours. Continue as from step 5.

40g (1½ oz) butter, plus
   extra for greasing
40g (1½ oz) plain flour
300ml (½ pint) milk
salt and freshly ground
   black pepper
100g (4 oz) feta cheese,
   cut into cubes
50g (2 oz) sun-blushed
   tomatoes, finely chopped

3 eggs, separated
25g (1 oz) Parmesan or
   Parmesan-style hard
   cheese, freshly grated
500ml (18 fl oz) tomato
   passata, seasoned
   with a few drops of
   Worcestershire sauce
1–2 tablespoons chopped
   fresh chives

Generously butter and base-line 6 × size 1 (150ml/¼ pint) ramekins. Preheat the oven to 220°C/Fan 200°C/Gas 7.

**1** Melt the butter in a generously sized saucepan, remove from the heat and blend in the flour. Return to the heat, and cook the roux for 30 seconds, stirring all the time. Add the milk bit by bit and bring to the boil, stirring constantly. Simmer until the sauce is thick and smooth.

**2** Remove the pan from the heat and beat in some seasoning, the feta and the drained sun-blushed tomatoes. When these are well incorporated, stir in the egg yolks.

**3** Whisk the egg whites until stiff, and stir 1 tablespoon into the sauce to loosen the mixture. Carefully fold in the remaining egg white. Spoon into the prepared ramekins and place them in a small roasting tin.

**4** Pour boiling water into the tin to come halfway up the ramekins and cook in the preheated oven for 10 minutes, then turn them around and cook for a further 8–10 minutes until golden and springy to the touch. Leave to stand for 5 minutes in the ramekin dishes to shrink back.

**5** Butter a shallow gratin dish (large enough to hold the little soufflés so that they just do not touch) and sprinkle over half of the Parmesan. Pour the seasoned passata into the gratin dish.

**6** Run the blade of a small palette knife around the edges of the soufflés, unmould them carefully, and put them into the gratin dish. Sprinkle the remaining Parmesan over the surface.

**7** Return to the oven for about 10–15 minutes until golden and bubbling. Scatter over the chives to garnish.

**TO COOK IN THE AGA**
Bake the soufflés in the bain-marie on the grid shelf on the floor of the Roasting Oven for 15–20 minutes. After 10 minutes, when the soufflés are a perfect golden brown, turn around if necessary and slide the cold shelf on the second set of runners and continue cooking until they are springy to the touch. Leave for 5 minutes in the dishes to shrink back. Continue with steps 5–7, baking in the Roasting Oven, but without the cold shelf, for another 15–20 minutes or until the soufflés are puffed up and golden.

# Sweet Pepper and Herb Dip

A quick and easy dip to make for pitta bread or raw vegetables, and it can also be used as a sauce for a cold cooked chicken salad. Jars of red peppers are available in all good supermarkets or, of course, you could skin a fresh pepper and use that instead. If you do not have a food processor, chop the herbs and red pepper by hand and mix with the other ingredients.

**TO PREPARE AHEAD**
Prepare ahead, and keep covered in the fridge for about 1 week.

**TO FREEZE**
Not suitable.

leaves from a large
  bunch of fresh parsley
leaves from a large
  bunch of fresh basil
100g (4 oz) red pepper,
  from a jar (½ × 225g jar)
juice of 1 lemon
1 tablespoon caster sugar

1 × 200g tub full-fat
  Greek yoghurt
200g (7 oz) 'light' low-calorie
  mayonnaise
150g (5 oz) full-fat cream
  cheese (e.g. Philadelphia)
salt and freshly ground
  black pepper

**1** Process the parsley and basil until coarsely chopped in a food processor.

**2** Add the red pepper, lemon juice and sugar and whiz for 30 seconds.

**3** Add the yoghurt, mayonnaise, cream cheese and salt and pepper. Whiz again, check the seasoning and serve.

# Homemade Garlic Herb Cheese

This cheese is so easy and yet so delicious, and, if you grow your own herbs,
it is cheap, too. Parsley, basil and chives are essential, but you can omit
the others if preferred, or if they are unavailable.

a small bunch of fresh parsley
3 sprigs of fresh basil
2 sprigs of fresh thyme
1 sprig of fresh tarragon
a small bunch of fresh chives
about 350g (12 oz) rich
   cream cheese

1–2 small garlic cloves,
   crushed
a little single cream
salt and freshly ground
   black pepper

**TO PREPARE AHEAD**
Prepare, cover and
keep in the fridge
for 2–3 days.

**TO FREEZE**
Not suitable.

**1** Take the stalks off the parsley and discard. Remove
the leaves from the stems of the other herbs. Snip the
chives finely.

**2** Put the parsley, basil, thyme and tarragon leaves
in a food processor and chop finely. Add the cheese
and garlic, thin down with a little cream and season.
Mix in the chives.

**3** Serve on the cheese board or use for recipes. Good
spread thinly on crostini.

# Garlic-stuffed Grilled Mussels

Choose the large, green-lipped New Zealand mussels for this dish if available. They look stunning and are less fiddly than the blue-grey mussels. If you can't easily get hold of them, use smaller shelled mussels and place them in a shallow ovenproof dish before covering with breadcrumbs and grilling.

**COOK NOW
EAT LATER**

## TO PREPARE AHEAD
Prepare to the end of step 5 up to 6 hours ahead. Cover and keep in the fridge until needed. Grill to serve until piping hot right through.

## TO FREEZE
Not suitable.

## TO COOK IN THE AGA
Arrange the stuffed mussels on a baking sheet and slide on to the second set of runners in the Roasting Oven for about 10 minutes or until golden brown and crisp.

1kg (2¼ lb) green-lipped
   New Zealand mussels
   (about 36)
about 50ml (2 fl oz) water
   or white wine
a knob of butter
1 small onion,
   finely chopped
2 garlic cloves, crushed
3 fresh tomatoes

about 75g (3 oz) fresh
   white breadcrumbs
finely grated zest of 1 lemon
2 tablespoons chopped
   fresh parsley
salt and freshly ground
   black pepper
about 25g (1 oz)
   Parmesan, grated

**1** If the mussels need cooking, wash in plenty of cold water, scraping away any barnacles and pulling off the beards. Discard any mussels that are open and which do not close when tapped sharply. Put the mussels and water or wine into a large pan, cover and cook over a high heat for 3–4 minutes, shaking the pan occasionally, until the mussels have just opened. (Discard any that remain closed.) Drain the mussels, then break off and discard the empty half shells. Put the mussels still in the outer shell in a single layer on a baking tray.

**2** Melt the butter in a small pan, add the onion and garlic and cook gently until soft but not coloured.

**3** Skin the tomatoes, cut in half, remove the seeds and chop the flesh finely.

**4** Mix the breadcrumbs with the onion and garlic, tomato, lemon zest, parsley and season with salt and pepper.

**5** Top each mussel with about a teaspoon of stuffing and sprinkle with Parmesan.

**6** Grill under a hot preheated grill for about 3–5 minutes, or until they are crisp and golden brown. Serve immediately on a bed of dressed fresh baby spinach.

# Crab Cakes
## with Mild Chilli Sauce

Fresh and frozen crabmeat can be difficult to come by, so I use tinned.
I would always make these cakes ahead and reheat them so that there
is no last-minute frying. Serve 2 crab cakes each as a first course.

450g (1 lb) fresh white
crabmeat, or 3 × 170g
cans white crabmeat,
drained
2 tablespoons chopped
fresh parsley
40g (1½ oz) cream crackers,
finely crushed in a
polythene bag with
a rolling pin
1 egg
2 tablespoons 'light'
low-calorie mayonnaise

1–2 teaspoons Dijon mustard
2 tablespoons lemon juice
1 tablespoon sweet chilli
dipping sauce
salt and freshly ground
black pepper
a little sunflower oil
for frying

**Mild Chilli Sauce**
8 tablespoons sweet
chilli dipping sauce
4 tablespoons crème fraîche

**COOK NOW
EAT LATER**

**TO PREPARE AHEAD**
Fry the crab cakes
the day before, then
reheat them, uncovered,
in an oven preheated
to 200°C/Fan 180°C/
Gas 6 for about
10 minutes or until
hot right through.

**TO FREEZE**
The crab cakes do not
freeze particularly well.

**TO COOK IN THE AGA**
Fry the crab cakes
ahead on the Boiling
Plate, then reheat
them, uncovered, on
non-stick paper on the
second set of runners
in the Roasting Oven
for about 7–10 minutes
until hot right through.

**1** Measure the crabmeat into a bowl and mix with
the parsley and cream crackers.

**2** Break the egg into a small bowl and whisk in the
mayonnaise, mustard, lemon juice and chilli sauce
and season with salt and pepper. Fold most of this
mixture into the crabmeat but try not to break up
the lumps of meat too much (you may not need all
the egg mixture – mix only until it binds together).
Taste and add more seasoning if necessary.

**3** Shape the mixture into 12 patties, put them on a
plate, cover with clingfilm and chill for at least 1 hour.

**4** Heat the sunflower oil in a large frying pan and
cook the crab cakes for 2–3 minutes until hot all the
way through, crisp and richly golden, turning once.
(These can be served straightaway.)

**5** Mix the sweet chilli sauce and crème fraîche and
keep in the fridge until needed. Serve a spoonful of
the sauce on the side of the plate with the crab cakes.

# Individual Baked Artichoke and Parma Ham Galettes

This artichoke recipe is Ann Usher's, an inspirational cook who now lives in France, and she gives it to her many guests from England. I have added a puff pastry case, but one with no bottom, which makes it wonderfully light. Dead easy, the pastry case is cut from ready-rolled puff pastry.

COOK NOW
EAT LATER

**TO PREPARE AHEAD**
Drain and cut the artichokes, and cover. Mix together the ham, fromage frais, Tabasco, Gruyère and seasoning, and cover. Cut the squares of pastry, stamp out the circles, put on the prepared baking trays, and cover tightly. Store everything overnight in the fridge. Assemble up to 6 hours ahead.

**TO FREEZE**
Not suitable.

**TO COOK IN THE AGA**
Bake on the floor of the Roasting Oven for about 7–10 minutes until the pastry is risen and golden brown.

1 × 285g jar seasoned artichoke hearts in oil
50–75g (2–3 oz) sliced dry-cured ham (Parma, Black Forest, Serrano or Bayonne)
1 × 250g tub full-fat fromage frais
4 drops Tabasco sauce
100g (4 oz) Gruyère cheese, grated

salt and freshly ground black pepper
1 × 375g packet ready-rolled puff pastry
a little milk
paprika

**To Serve**
1 small packet rocket leaves
olive oil
balsamic vinegar

Well grease a large baking tray or line a baking tray with non-stick paper. Preheat the oven to 220°C/Fan 200°C/Gas 7.

**1** Drain the artichoke hearts in a colander then on kitchen paper to mop up all the oil. Cut the artichokes so that you have 24 pieces, 3 pieces to put into each pastry case.

**2** Cut the ham into small pieces. Mix these with the fromage frais, Tabasco and two-thirds of the Gruyère. Season to taste with salt and pepper.

**3** Unroll the pastry on to a lightly floured surface and cut into 8 rectangles. Stamp a 5cm (2 in) circle out from the centre of each pastry square. Lift each square on to the prepared baking tray. Brush the pastry with milk.

**4** Put 3 pieces of artichoke in the centre circles of the pastry squares, and top with the fromage frais mixture, piling it up slightly. Sprinkle the reserved cheese over the artichokes and the pastry then dust with paprika.

**5** Bake in the preheated oven for about 15–20 minutes or until the pastry is risen and golden brown.

**6** Serve at once with rocket salad, dressed with a little olive oil and balsamic vinegar.

# Miniature Bangers and Mash

Rather than boiling only 2 small potatoes to fill the sausages, why not boil extra and use the leftovers for supper. Don't forget to warn the guests if the sausages are very hot. When making food for a drinks party, don't forget old favourites like devils-on-horseback (prunes wrapped in bacon). Some supermarkets sell ready-cooked cocktail sausages and they are also wonderful served with equal quantities of runny honey and mustard. Reheat as below and coat over the sausages while hot!

**COOK NOW
EAT LATER**

20 cocktail pork sausages
mashed potatoes
salt and freshly
    ground black pepper

grated Parmesan
paprika (optional)

**TO PREPARE AHEAD**
Prepare to the end of step 4 up to 1 day before. Cover and keep in the fridge. Continue with step 5.

**TO FREEZE**
At the end of step 4, pack the sausages in a single layer in a ridged freezer container. Freeze for up to 1 month. Thaw for about 2 hours at room temperature before reheating as in step 5.

**TO COOK IN THE AGA**
Cook the sausages on non-stick paper in a roasting tin on the floor of the Roasting Oven until cooked and brown. Reheat in the Roasting Oven on the top set of runners for about 5 minutes.

**1** Grill the sausages (if raw), turning once or twice, until cooked and evenly brown. Allow the sausages to become completely cold as it is then easier to make a slit down the length to form an opening.

Preheat the oven to 200°C/Fan 180°F/Gas 6.

**2** Ensure that the mashed potatoes are very well seasoned. Fill into a piping bag fitted with a plain narrow nozzle. (You can also spoon the potato into the sausage.)

**3** Hold a sausage, squeezing the ends gently together, and pipe or spoon some potato into the gap. Continue with all 20 sausages.

**4** Arrange them on to a baking tray and sprinkle with Parmesan and dust with paprika, if using.

**5** Reheat in the preheated oven for about 10 minutes or until piping hot.

# Cocktail Toad in the Hole

Loved by both children and grown-ups! A wonderful
way to use up leftover cocktail sausages.

36 cocktail pork sausages
100g (4 oz) plain flour
2 eggs
1 egg yolk
250ml (8 fl oz) milk

vegetable oil (optional)
creamed horseradish,
    mustard or mango
    chutney (optional)

Preheat the oven to 220°C/Fan 200°C/Gas 7. You will
need 3 × 12-hole tins.

**1** Grill the sausages until completely cooked and golden
brown (or buy them ready cooked).

**2** Measure the flour into a bowl, make a well in the centre
of the flour and blend in the eggs and yolk with a little
of the milk. Whisk to a smooth paste. Blend in the
remaining milk to make a batter, and whisk really
well until smooth.

**3** Add a drop of oil (or fat from the sausages) into each
hole. Slide the tins into the preheated oven to heat the
fat. When the fat is smoking, drop a cooked sausage
into the bottom of each hole and pour over the smooth
batter. Return to the oven and bake for about 12–15
minutes until the batter is risen and golden brown.
Check underneath one of the 'toads' – it should be
golden brown.

**4** Spoon a tiny amount of horseradish, mustard or
mango chutney on to each sausage before serving,
if liked. Allow to cool slightly, but serve warm.

**TO PREPARE AHEAD**
The sausages can be
cooked up to 3 days
ahead, cooled and
kept in the fridge. The
completed 'toads' can
be made up to 14 hours
ahead and reheated for
about 5 minutes in the
oven at 200°C/Fan
180°C/Gas 6 until
hot right through.

**TO FREEZE**
Not suitable.

**TO COOK IN THE AGA**
Cook the sausages on
non-stick paper in a
roasting tin on the
floor of the Roasting
Oven until cooked and
brown. Heat the oil
on the second set of
runners in the Roasting
Oven and bake the
'toads' until well risen
and golden brown,
about 12–15 minutes.
If reheating, do so in
the Roasting Oven on
the grid shelf on the
floor for about 5 minutes
until piping hot.

COOK NOW, EAT LATER

✹

# Fish

CHAPTER TWO

Fish is notorious for cooking quickly, for needing to be done at the last minute, for not 'lasting' very well when kept hot, and for not freezing. But even fish, if you have bought the best quality, can be prepared in advance to a certain extent. A number of the recipes here require marination, and then the fish is cooked at the last moment. Other recipes suggest searing one side of the fish in advance, and then you only need to cook it for a few minutes before serving. Another huge advantage of this advance searing is that you get rid of any fishy smells before your guests arrive.

Fish must always be extremely fresh, though, and the major clue to freshness is smell. It must not smell too fishy. You should ideally buy fish on the day you are going to prepare it, and this ought to be either the day of cooking or the day before. The other major factor when dealing with fish is that it must not be overcooked. Fish is translucent at first, and is cooked when it becomes opaque. Marginally undercook if you are going to keep fish warm (as is usual when feeding guests), as the fish will continue to cook slightly.

A lot of people are put off cooking fish because they feel that it all has to be done at the last minute, getting themselves, the kitchen and even the rest of the house, smelling of fish. This need not be so if you think – and cook – ahead.

# Baked Sole Florentine

A wonderfully easy fish recipe which takes very little time to cook. Lemon sole fillets are quite expensive, but you can keep the cost down by choosing small fish Ask the fishmonger to skin and fillet 6 fish for you. Serve with lemon wedges.

**COOK NOW EAT LATER**

### TO PREPARE AHEAD
Prepare to the end of step 3. Cover and keep in the fridge for up to 1 day.

### TO FREEZE
Not suitable.

### TO COOK IN THE AGA
Bake at the top of the Roasting Oven for about 10–15 minutes until the fish flesh is white and firm and cooked through. The baking time may alter according to the depth of dish used.

25g (1 oz) butter, plus extra for greasing
salt and freshly ground black pepper
1 medium onion, finely chopped
225g (8 oz) fresh young spinach, washed and finely shredded

a little freshly grated nutmeg
12 lemon sole fillets, skinned
200ml (7 fl oz) double cream
2 tablespoons coarsley grated Parmesan
paprika
lemon wedges to serve

Butter and season a shallow ovenproof dish large enough to take the fish. Preheat the oven to 200°C/Fan 180°C/Gas 6.

**1** Melt the butter in a large frying pan, add the onion and cook over a low heat for 10–15 minutes until soft. Add the spinach and cook over a high heat for a few minutes until it has wilted and all the water has been driven off. Season with salt, pepper and nutmeg. Remove from the heat and allow to cool completely.

**2** Press the spinach mixture with a kitchen towel to remove any excess moisture.

**3** Meanwhile, season the fish with salt and pepper on both sides and arrange the 6 largest fillets skinned side down in the prepared oven dish. Divide the spinach mixture and place in the middle of each fillet. Using a sharp knife cut a slit about 5cm (2 in) long in the centre of each of the remaining 6 fillets. Position the top fillet over the spinach and bottom fillet, allowing the filling to just show through.

**4** Season the cream with salt and pepper and pour over the fillets. Sprinkle with Parmesan and dust with paprika.

**5** Bake in the preheated oven for about 25–30 minutes until the fish flesh is white and firm and cooked through.

# Baked Cod
## with Pesto and Parmesan Mash

An all-in-one dish that can be prepared ahead. This could also be made with salmon fillets. Serve with a green salad or petits pois.

**TO PREPARE AHEAD**
If the fish is very fresh and the mashed potato cold, you may cover the assembled uncooked fish and store in the fridge for up to 1 day.

**TO FREEZE**
Not suitable.

**TO COOK IN THE AGA**
Bake on the top set of runners of the Roasting Oven for about 10–15 minutes until the fish has turned white.

about 500g (1 lb 2 oz) main-crop potatoes, peeled
a good knob of butter
a little milk
6 teaspoons pesto
salt and freshly ground black pepper
6 × 175g (6 oz) tail fillets of cod, skinned

6 large tomatoes, skinned, seeded and cut into long strips
a few sprigs of fresh basil, chopped
75g (3 oz) Parmesan, coarsely grated

Lightly grease a large baking tray. Preheat the oven to 220°C/Fan 200°C/Gas 7.

**1** Bring the potatoes to the boil in salted water, cover and simmer for about 15–20 minutes or until tender. Drain well, then mash, adding butter, a little milk, the pesto and some seasoning.

**2** Season the cod fillets on both sides, then place on the greased baking tray. Divide the mashed potato and spread or roughly pipe on to each fillet. Mix the strips of tomato and basil together, season and arrange over the mash. Sprinkle with Parmesan.

**3** Bake in the preheated oven for about 15 minutes or until the fish has turned white. Serve immediately.

# Salmon Tranche
## with Fresh Lime and Ginger Sauce

Char-grilling or frying fish is a smelly, smoky business, and to do this earlier in the day – or even the day before – is a huge advantage. Then all you have to do is blast the fish in the oven for a few minutes, and make a quick sauce.

**COOK NOW
EAT LATER**

**TO PREPARE AHEAD**
Marinate the salmon for a few hours or overnight. At step 4 brown the salmon quickly on one side, lift out, cool quickly, cover and keep in the fridge until ready to cook. You can do this the night before. To serve, arrange the fillets in an ovenproof serving dish, grilled side up, and reheat in the preheated oven at 200°C/Fan 180°C/Gas 6 for about 6–10 minutes. To test when done, check to see the fish is cooked through (or almost, if keeping it warm). Quickly make the sauce using the marinade, butter and chives before serving.

6 × 150g (5 oz) salmon fillets (cut from the centre of the salmon), skinned
finely grated zest and juice of 2 limes
1 × 5cm (1 in) piece fresh ginger root, grated

6 tablespoons dark soy sauce
freshly ground black pepper
225g (8 oz) butter
3 tablespoons chopped fresh chives

**1** Check that the salmon is without any small bones. (The easiest way to remove any is with tweezers.)

**2** Put the zest and juice of the limes, the ginger and soy sauce into a bowl. Season the salmon with pepper and turn in the marinade in the bowl. Cover with clingfilm, and leave to marinate in the fridge for a few hours or overnight.

**3** Lift the fish out of the marinade, pat the top dry with kitchen paper and spread with a little of the butter. Strain the marinade into a small jug.

**4** Preheat a ridged grill pan over a high heat on the hob for a few moments. When very hot add the salmon, butter side down, and char-grill until golden, about 1 minute. Lower the heat and continue to cook the salmon until it is just cooked through, 6–10 minutes, depending on the thickness of the fish. Lift out and keep warm.

**5** Next quickly make the sauce and glaze. Pour the marinade into a pan, bring to the boil then whisk in knobs of the remaining butter until it has all been included. Stir with a wooden spoon over a high heat for a few moments until shining. No need to season. Take care not to reduce too much.

**6** Arrange a fish fillet on each plate. Add the chives to the sauce and spoon some sauce over one end of the fish. Serve with a green vegetable.

**TO FREEZE**
Not suitable.

**TO COOK IN THE AGA**
Brown the salmon in a hot frying pan or ridged grill pan for 1 minute on one side on the Boiling Plate. Transfer to a roasting tin, grilled side up. Bake the salmon on the grid shelf on the floor of the Roasting Oven for about 8 minutes or until the fish is a matt pale pink all through.

# Teriyaki Tuna

It is worthwhile buying a good-quality marinade. If overcooked, tuna can be dry, but this marinade helps to keep it moist.

**COOK NOW EAT LATER**

## TO PREPARE AHEAD

Marinate the tuna ahead. Keep in the fridge overnight or until needed.

## TO FREEZE

Not suitable.

## TO COOK IN THE AGA

Cook the tuna in a preheated pan on the Boiling Plate, followed by the ingredients for the sauce.

6 × 175g (6 oz) fresh tuna steaks, about 2.5cm (1 in) thick
100ml (4 fl oz) teriyaki marinade (buy in a bottle)
1 × 2.5cm (1 in) piece fresh root ginger, finely grated

1 tablespoon clear honey
6 spring onions, finely sliced
2 tablespoons sunflower oil
1 red pepper, seeded and finely sliced

**1** Put the tuna steaks into a shallow, non-metallic dish. Mix together the teriyaki marinade, ginger, honey and spring onions and pour over the tuna steaks. Cover and leave to marinate in the fridge for a few hours, turning once.

**2** Heat the oil in a large non-stick frying pan. When very hot, add the tuna steaks and cook for about 2–3 minutes on each side, depending on the thickness. Lift out and keep warm.

**3** Add the red pepper to the pan and stir-fry quickly. Pour in the marinade with about 200ml (7 fl oz) water, and bring to the boil. Boil until of a thin syrupy consistency.

**4** Lift the slices of red pepper from the sauce with a slotted spoon and spoon on top of the tuna steaks to garnish. Offer the remaining sauce separately. Serve with boiled rice and a green salad.

# Rigatoni Pasta Bake
## with Tuna and Two Cheeses

Rigatoni are large tube-shaped pasta, ideal for use in a baked pasta dish.

**TO PREPARE AHEAD**

Prepare to the end of step 3 up to 24 hours ahead. Cool, cover and keep in the fridge. Complete steps 4 and 5 to serve.

**TO FREEZE**

Add 75ml (⅛ pint) more milk to the cheese sauce if you wish to freeze the pasta bake after step 3. Don't pour over the cream or scatter with the cheese yet. Cover and freeze for up to 1 month. Thaw overnight in the fridge. Complete step 4 and heat as in step 5, increasing the time to about 40 minutes, or until piping hot.

**TO COOK IN THE AGA**

Bake the assembled dish on the grid shelf on the floor of the Roasting Oven for about 25 minutes.

1 small onion, coarsely chopped
175g (6 oz) dried rigatoni
1 × 400g can tuna in brine, drained well
1–2 tablespoons capers, drained and roughly chopped
1 tablespoon snipped fresh chives
2 large tomatoes, about 200g (7 oz), skinned, seeded and chopped
salt and freshly ground black pepper
75ml (⅛ pint) double cream

**Cheese Sauce**
50g (2 oz) butter
50g (2 oz) plain flour
about 600ml (1 pint) milk
1 teaspoon Dijon mustard
2 tablespoons finely chopped fresh parsley
25g (1 oz) mozzarella cheese, grated
25g (1 oz) Gruyère cheese, grated

Preheat the oven to 200°C/Fan 180°C/Gas 6. You will need a 28 × 23 × 5cm (11 × 9 × 2 in) shallow ovenproof dish, lightly buttered.

**1** Cook the onion in boiling salted water with the pasta until al dente. Drain and refresh with cold water until completely cold. Drain well then place in the prepared ovenproof dish.

**2** Next make the sauce. Melt the butter in a large pan, take off the heat and stir in the flour. Gradually add the milk, stirring continuously, and bring to the boil. Season with salt, pepper and mustard, and simmer for 2 minutes. Add the parsley and half of each cheese. Stir to mix.

**3** Mix the tuna, capers, chives and tomatoes in a bowl and season well with salt and pepper. Spoon the tuna mixture over the pasta in the dish, spreading it out evenly. Pour the cheese sauce over the top. Finally pour over the cream and scatter with the remaining cheeses.

**4** Bake in the preheated oven for about 30 minutes until the top is golden and bubbling.

SERVES 6

# Char-grilled Sea Bass
## on a Bed of Vegetables

Supper in one dish. Prepare the vegetables and fish ahead,
leaving only a salad to make on the day.

butter
4 red peppers, cut in half
  and seeds removed
700g (1½ lb) new potatoes
1 large onion, cut into wedges
olive oil
1 garlic clove, crushed
salt and freshly ground
  black pepper

4 large tomatoes, skinned,
  quartered and seeded
50g (2 oz) black olives
  in oil, drained
6 sea bass fillets, with
  the skin left on
chopped fresh parsley
  and basil

**TO PREPARE AHEAD**
Prepare the vegetables
ahead to the end of step
4. Keep in a cool place
until needed. Scar the
skin of the fish for
1 minute, as in step 5.
Remove to a plate and
chill until ready to cook
(this could be done the
night before). Keep them
separate. Reheat and
cook as in steps 6 and 7.

**TO FREEZE**
Not suitable.

Lightly butter a 25 × 38cm (10 × 15 in) ovenproof
dish. Preheat the oven to 200°C/Fan 180°C/Gas 6,
and preheat the grill.

**1** Put the peppers cut side down on to the grill rack
and place under the hot grill until the skin blisters
and blackens. Whilst still hot, put the peppers into
a polythene bag and seal the top so that they sweat.

**2** Meanwhile, boil the potatoes and onion in salted
water until the potatoes are only just done. Drain
and cut the potatoes into even pieces about 2.5cm (1 in)
square, or a bit smaller. Return to the pan with the onion,
1–2 tablespoons of the oil, the garlic, salt and pepper.

**3** Arrange the potatoes and onion down the centre of
a large ovenproof dish, scatter the tomatoes on top,
and season with salt and pepper.

**4** When the peppers are cool enough to handle, peel off
the skin and cut the flesh into quarters. Mix with the
olives, season and coat with olive oil. Spoon the peppers
and olives down either side of the potatoes. Cover with foil.

*Recipe continued overleaf*

## TO COOK IN THE AGA

Char-grill the fish ahead, skin side down in a ridged grill pan, on the Boiling Plate for about 1 minute until the skin is crisp and brown. About 25 minutes before serving, reheat the vegetables on the floor of the Roasting Oven for about 20 minutes. Put the fish on top of the potatoes, skin side up, and roast at the top of the Roasting Oven for 8 minutes until just cooked.

## TIP

Try to always have some chopped fresh parsley in the fridge, as it makes all the difference to the look of a dish. Pack tightly into a mug covered with clingfilm, with a couple of holes pierced in the top, and it will keep fresh for a good few days.

*Recipe continued*

**5** Slash the fish skin and brush with a little oil. Season the fish and fry skin side down in a very hot frying pan or ridged grill pan over high heat for about 1 minute until the skin is crisp and brown. The flesh will still be raw underneath.

**6** Reheat the vegetables, covered, in the preheated oven for about 20 minutes, until very steamy and exceedingly hot. Remove the foil.

**7** Put the fish on top of the potatoes, skin side up, and bake for about 8–10 minutes until just cooked. Sprinkle with parsley and basil to serve.

# Moroccan Fish

Use monkfish if you prefer. Harissa paste is a hot
chilli paste used in North African dishes.

**COOK NOW
EAT LATER**

## TO PREPARE AHEAD

Cook the sauce to the
end of step 3 but only for
20 minutes. Cool, cover
and keep in the fridge for
up to 24 hours. Marinate
the fish a few hours
ahead, cover and keep
in the fridge. Reheat the
sauce very gently over a
low heat, then continue
with step 5.

## TO FREEZE

Cool the sauce at the
end of step 3, pack
and freeze for up to
3 months. Thaw
overnight at cool room
temperature, bring
back to the boil and
bubble for 3–4 minutes
then use to complete
the recipe. Do not
freeze the fish and
sauce together.

## TO COOK IN THE AGA

At step 2, cook the
onions covered in the
Simmering Oven for
about 10–15 minutes.
At step 5, bring to the
boil, cover and transfer
to the Simmering Oven
for about 15–20 minutes.

2 tablespoons olive oil
350g (12 oz) small
 courgettes, roughly cubed
450g (1 lb) red onions,
 roughly chopped
3 level teaspoons
 harissa paste
1 × 400g can chopped
 tomatoes
500ml (18 fl oz)
 tomato passata

1kg (2¼ lb) skinless cod loin,
 cut into large pieces
1 × 400g can chickpeas,
 drained
50g (2 oz) black olives,
 stoned
salt and freshly ground
 black pepper
2 tablespoons each of chopped
 fresh coriander and parsley

**1** First make the sauce. Heat the olive oil in a large
frying pan (one with a lid) or shallow casserole dish,
add the courgettes and fry over a high heat for
10 minutes until golden. Lift out with a slotted
spoon and transfer to a bowl.

**2** Add the onions to the pan and fry for 10 minutes
until beginning to colour. Stir 2 teaspoons of harissa
paste into the onions and cook for a further 2–3 minutes.

**3** Return the courgettes to the pan, then mix in the
chopped tomatoes and tomato passata. Bring to the
boil, cover, then simmer gently for about 30 minutes.

**4** Marinate the fish with the remaining harissa
paste, as the sauce is cooking.

Preheat the oven to 200°C/Fan 180°C/Gas 6.

**5** Add the marinated fish to the casserole with the
chickpeas and olives. Push the fish down into the
sauce, season with salt and pepper, cover and cook
in the preheated oven for 15–20 minutes. The fish
should be white rather than opaque.

**6** When cooked, gently stir the coriander and parsley
into the sauce and serve with rice or couscous.

# Chilli-hot Monkfish Pasta
## with Vegetables

Billingsgate Market has a brilliant training school for young fishmongers.
This is an adaptation of a recipe the chef made us. Buy young
mangetout and tiny fine beans.

700g (1½ lb) monkfish,
  skinned and cut into
  2cm (¾ in) pieces
5 tablespoons chilli
  dipping sauce
350g (12 oz) dried pasta shells
400g (14 oz) fine French
  beans, cut into 3
350g (12 oz) mangetout,
  cut diagonally

1–2 tablespoons olive oil
1 onion, finely chopped
2 garlic cloves, crushed
200ml (7 fl oz) white wine
4 tablespoons hoisin sauce
6 tablespoons crème fraîche
salt and freshly ground
  black pepper

**COOK NOW
EAT LATER**

**1** Put the monkfish in a bowl, pour over the chilli dipping
sauce and stir.

**2** Cook the pasta in boiling, generously salted water
until just cooked al dente. Refresh in plenty of
running cold water.

**3** Blanch the beans for 3 minutes in boiling salted water,
add the mangetout and continue to blanch for another
30 seconds. Drain and refresh in cold water.

**4** Heat the oil in a large pan and sauté the onion and
garlic without colouring until soft. Add the wine and
reduce to 3 tablespoons. Toss in the monkfish, stir for
1 minute, then add the pasta and vegetables. Heat for
a few minutes, stirring continually, then add the hoisin
sauce and the crème fraîche. Season and serve
immediately while everything is piping hot.

### TO PREPARE AHEAD
Marinate the monkfish
in the chilli dipping
sauce up to 8 hours
ahead, keeping in the
fridge. Cook the pasta,
drain, refresh in cold
water, drain again and
cover with clingfilm.
Blanch the beans and
mangetout, as directed,
drain, refresh and drain
again. Cook the pasta
and vegetables up to 6
hours ahead and reheat
in boiling water at the
last minute.

### TO FREEZE
Not suitable.

### TO COOK IN THE AGA
Sauté the onion and
garlic on the Boiling
Plate, and then transfer
to the Simmering Oven
until soft, about 10–15
minutes. Continue step
4 on the Boiling Plate
as directed.

# Fresh Tuna Steaks
## on a Bed of Lentils

I used to make this with swordfish steaks but there are now concerns about
its sustainability. The recipe is just as good with fresh tuna steaks,
and you cook them in the same way, too.

**COOK NOW
EAT LATER**

## TO PREPARE AHEAD

The lentils can be made
up to 12 hours ahead.
Fry the steaks for about
45–60 seconds on one
side – this can be done
12 hours ahead – then
cool and keep in the
fridge. To serve, arrange
the lentils in a dish large
enough to hold the 6
steaks, cover with foil
and reheat in an oven
preheated to 200°C/
Fan 180°C/Gas 6 for
15–20 minutes. Remove
the foil, put the steaks
on top (browned side
up) and cook for 10–15
minutes (depending
on the thickness) until
cooked but not dry.

## TO FREEZE

Not suitable.

## TO COOK IN THE AGA

Cook the onion covered
in the Simmering Oven
for 15 minutes. Finish
step 2 on the Simmering
Plate. Fry the steaks
on the Boiling Plate.

250g (9 oz) dried Puy lentils
1.1 litres (2 pints) stock,
  or water and stock cube
salt and freshly ground
  black pepper
2 teaspoons fresh thyme leaves
2 tablespoons olive oil, plus
  extra for greasing
1 large onion, chopped
200g (7 oz) oyster mushrooms,
  thickly sliced
4–5 tomatoes, skinned, seeded
  and cut into neat strips

3 tablespoons coarsely
  chopped fresh parsley
6 × 150–175g (5–6 oz)
  fresh tuna steaks

**To Serve**
a little olive oil and
  balsamic vinegar
  mixed together (optional)
chopped fresh parsley

**1** Rinse the lentils, drain, and bring to the boil in a pan
with the stock or water and stock cube, with a little salt
and pepper and the thyme. Simmer uncovered for about
15–20 minutes until just soft. Drain and set aside.

**2** Heat the oil in a large frying pan, add the onion after
a few minutes, cover and soften over a low heat for about
15 minutes. When soft, add the mushrooms and fry over
a high heat for about 2 minutes. Season well with salt
and pepper. Add the lentils, tomatoes and parsley to
the pan and check the seasoning.

**3** Heat a ridged grill pan or large frying pan over a high
heat until very hot. Lightly oil and season the fish steaks
on both sides. Brown the steaks for about 2–3 minutes
on each side, depending on the thickness.

**4** Spoon the hot lentil mixture into a hot serving dish
(or on to individual plates) and serve the swordfish steaks
on top. Spoon about a teaspoon of balsamic vinegar and
olive oil over the top of each steak, if using, and garnish
with parsley to serve.

# Salmon Coulibiac

Make the rice and salmon mixture some time ahead if it suits you. Leave covered in the fridge overnight then assemble the coulibiac on the day it is being eaten.

175g (6 oz) long grain rice and wild rice
300ml (½ pint) water
1 teaspoon salt
50g (2 oz) butter
1 large Spanish onion, chopped
175g (6 oz) button mushrooms, quartered
salt and freshly ground black pepper

450g (1 lb) salmon fillet, skinned
2 good tablespoons chopped fresh parsley

**To Assemble**
1 × 270g packet filo pastry, about 6 sheets
about 50g (2 oz) butter, melted

**COOK NOW EAT LATER**

**TO PREPARE AHEAD**
Prepare the rice and salmon mixture up to 24 hours before, cool quickly and keep covered in the fridge. Assemble the coulibiac the day it is being eaten, up to 12 hours ahead.

**TO FREEZE**
Not suitable.

**TIP**
If buying the rice separately, use 150g (5 oz) long grain rice and 25g (1 oz) wild rice, and cook according to the packet instructions.

Lightly grease a baking tray. Preheat the oven to 200°C/ Fan 180°C/Gas 6.

**1** Measure the rice into a pan and add the water and salt. Bring to the boil, cover and simmer gently for about 15 minutes until the rice is tender and the liquid has been absorbed.

**2** Melt the butter in a medium pan, add the onion and cook gently for about 10 minutes, until the onion is soft. Add the mushrooms to the pan and toss over a high heat for a few moments. Season with salt and pepper.

**3** Cut the salmon into two pieces if necessary so that it will fit into the pan in a single layer. Add the salmon to the onion and mushrooms, cover and simmer gently for about 10 minutes until the salmon is cooked. Flake the fish into fairly large pieces – this can be done still in the pan. Add to the rice and stir in the parsley. Mix well, adjust seasoning and allow to cool.

*Recipe continued overleaf*

COOK NOW
EAT LATER

## TO COOK IN THE AGA

Bring the rice to the boil in 250ml (9 fl oz) water on the Boiling Plate, cover and put into the Simmering Oven for about 15 minutes until tender. Cook the onion, covered, in the Simmering Oven for about 15–20 minutes until tender. Add the mushrooms and the salmon, and return to the Simmering Oven, covered, until the fish flakes and is opaque. Bake the assembled coulibiac on a baking sheet on the floor of the Roasting Oven until golden, about 20–25 minutes. You may need to slide the cold sheet in on the second set of runners if it's getting too brown.

*Recipe continued*

**4** Place 3 sheets of filo, slightly overlapping, side by side (about 30.5 × 38cm/12 × 15 in) on a baking sheet. Brush with most of the melted butter. Lay 3 more sheets on top. Spoon the filling down the centre of the filo (leaving large gaps at the side). Fold the pastry over the top and crimp the edges at the join. Squeeze the parcel so that it is long and thin and quite pointed at the top. Brush with a little more melted butter before cooking.

**5** Bake in the preheated oven for about 40 minutes until the filo is golden and crisp and the filling hot throughout. Serve with low-fat crème fraîche and a green salad.

COOK NOW **68** EAT LATER
FISH

# Salmon and Fennel Fish Pie

**SERVES 6**

This is a fish pie for a very special occasion. Adding ricotta cheese to the mashed potato lightens the texture and gives an interesting flavour.

**COOK NOW EAT LATER**

### TO PREPARE AHEAD

Prepare the pie to the end of step 4. Cover with clingfilm and keep in the fridge for up to 1 day. Follow step 5 to cook – it will take about 10 minutes longer cooking from cold.

### TO FREEZE

Not suitable.

350g (12 oz) fresh
  fennel bulbs
150ml (¼ pint) dry
  white wine
about 400ml (¾ pint)
  hot milk
50g (2 oz) butter
50g (2 oz) plain flour
salt and freshly
  ground black pepper
700g (1½ lb) salmon fillet,
  skinned and cut into
  1cm (½ in) pieces
1 tablespoon chopped
  fresh dill
4 eggs, hard boiled
  and cut into eighths

**Topping**
800g (1¾ lb) King Edward
  potatoes (weight before
  peeling), peeled and cut
  into large chunks
250g (9 oz) ricotta cheese
about 4 tablespoons milk
50g (2 oz) Parmesan,
  freshly grated

You will need one shallow ovenproof dish, capacity 2 litres (4 pints), about 35 × 25 × 5cm (14 × 10 × 2 in). Preheat the oven to 200°C/Fan 180°C/Gas 6.

**1** For the topping, cook the potatoes in boiling salted water until tender. Drain well.

**2** Whilst the potatoes are cooking, cut the fennel bulbs in half from top to bottom, and remove and discard the core. Cut into quarters and then slice in horseshoe shapes. Put into a small pan with the wine and simmer until the fennel is soft, about 10 minutes. Drain the fennel, reserving the liquid, and make up to 1 pint with the milk.

**3** Melt the butter in a medium pan, add the flour and stir to mix. Gradually add the milk and fennel liquid, stirring continuously, and allowing to thicken. Season well, bring to the boil and simmer for a few minutes.

**4** Add the salmon pieces and cook for a further few minutes. Stir in the fennel and dill, check the seasoning, and spread into the dish. Scatter the eggs over the top, pressing them down gently into the fish mixture.

**5** Mash the potatoes until smooth. Stir in the ricotta cheese, adding enough milk to give a creamy texture, and season with plenty of salt and pepper. Spoon over the fish and sauce, spreading the potatoes right to the edge of the dish. Sprinkle with the Parmesan.

**6** Bake in the preheated oven for about 30–35 minutes until cooked through, brown, crisp and piping hot.

**TO COOK IN THE AGA**
Bake the assembled dish on the grid shelf on the floor of the Roasting Oven for about 30 minutes until the potato is crisp and golden and the pie is piping hot.

# Phad Thai Noodles with Seafood

A healthy fresh recipe, inspired by my much-admired friend
Ken Hom, the king of Chinese and Eastern cooking.

**TO PREPARE AHEAD**
Chop all the vegetables,
cover and keep in the
fridge until needed,
up to 8 hours ahead.
Stir-fry just before
serving.

**TO FREEZE**
Not suitable.

**TO COOK IN THE AGA**
Boil the noodles and
stir-fry the vegetables
on the Boiling Plate.

175g (6 oz) Thai rice noodles
  or fine egg noodles
150g (5 oz) sugar-snap peas,
  cut thinly on the diagonal
2 tablespoons sunflower oil
1 garlic clove, crushed
1 × 2.5cm (1 in) piece fresh
  root ginger, finely grated
2 red chillies, seeded and
  finely chopped
150g (5 oz) shiitake
  mushrooms, sliced
1 leek, sliced lengthways
  into thin batons

100g (4 oz) baby sweetcorn,
  cut into 4 lengthways
100g (4 oz) beansprouts
350g (12 oz) mixed seafood
  (i.e. fresh prawns, scallops
  and squid)
2 tablespoons sherry
4 tablespoons soy sauce
2 tablespoons oyster sauce
2 tablespoons lime juice
a few salted peanuts
  (optional) and sliced
  spring onions to garnish

**1** Cook the noodles according to the packet instructions.
For the last minute add the sugar-snap peas to the noodle
pan. Drain and refresh lightly.

**2** Heat the oil in a large frying pan or wok over a high
heat until very hot. Add the garlic, ginger and chillies
and fry for 2–3 minutes. Add the mushrooms, leek, baby
corn and beansprouts and stir-fry for about 5 minutes.

**3** When the vegetables are nearly cooked, add the seafood
to the pan with the sherry, soy and oyster sauces and
lime juice.

**4** When the seafood is cooked through, stir in the noodles
and sugar-snap peas, and mix well over a low heat for
a few minutes.

**5** Turn into a serving dish and garnish with peanuts,
if using, and spring onions.

COOK NOW, EAT LATER

✦

# Poultry
# and Game

CHAPTER THREE

I have given you some interesting chicken recipes here, which are very international in flavour – from Chile and Spain to France and Thailand – plus a trio of duck and pheasant ideas. In all of them I have removed the skin, which makes the meat cook in a slightly different way. It also means that the final dish will contain much less fat, which many people prefer nowadays.

(Keep the bones and skin from poultry and game and use them for stock. And if you like duck 'crackling', simply cut the skin into strips and fry or bake until crisp.)

Overcooking is always a fear with prime poultry and game cuts, such as chicken and pheasant breasts. Although undercooking in advance is not generally considered to be sensible, provided you have bought best-quality meat and cool and chill it properly, this should not be a problem, and will be safe.

Several of the recipes here can be marinated or partially prepared in advance before being finished at the last moment. But most can be completely cooked at least the day before, then reheated until piping hot to serve. And of course a majority of them can be cooked well ahead and frozen. All you have to do then is defrost, reheat well, garnish and serve.

A primary consideration when cooking casserole-type dishes to be reheated from cold or frozen is the quantity of sauce. Some of the sauce can be lost through evaporation during reheating, and so we have taken this into account. Most people like a *lot* of sauce anyway.

Always remember to taste any dish in the kitchen before reheating after chilling or freezing: it's too late to add significant seasoning by the time you taste it at the table!

# Pan-fried Pheasant
## with a Mango Sauce

A quick way to cook pheasant breasts without allowing the pheasant to become dry.

olive oil
1 large onion, finely chopped
6 boneless pheasant breasts,
  skin removed
3 tablespoons mango chutney

3 tablespoons Worcestershire
  sauce
450ml (¾ pint) double cream
paprika
chopped fresh parsley

**COOK NOW EAT LATER**

Preheat the oven to 200°C/Fan 180°C/Gas 6.

**1** Heat 1 tablespoon of olive oil in a large sauté pan, fry the onion, lower the temperature, cover and cook gently until tender, about 10–15 minutes. Spread over the base of a shallow ovenproof dish.

**2** Pan-fry the pheasant breasts in a little more oil on a high heat on both sides until brown. Slice each breast into 3 slices on the diagonal, then put on top of the soft onion and season with salt and pepper. They should still be pink in the middle.

**3** Stir the mango chutney and Worcestershire sauce into the cream, season and pour over the pheasant. Dust with paprika and cook in the preheated oven for about 15–20 minutes until the pheasant is tender and the sauce is brown.

**4** Allow to rest for a few minutes, before scattering with parsley. Serve with mashed potatoes to mop up the sauce, and perhaps fresh broccoli.

### TO PREPARE AHEAD
Cook the onion and pan-fry the pheasant 1 day ahead until barely cooked. Cool, cover and keep separately in the fridge. Mix together the ingredients for the sauce, cover and keep in the fridge until needed. To serve, slice each breast into 3, put into the ovenproof dish and pour over the sauce. Reheat for about 20 minutes at the same temperature until piping hot and bubbling.

### TO FREEZE
Complete to the end of step 3. Cool quickly, pack and freeze for up to 2 months. Thaw and reheat as above.

### TO COOK IN THE AGA
Pan-fry the pheasant breasts on the Boiling Plate then continue with steps 2 and 3 towards the top of the Roasting Oven for about 10–15 minutes.

# Braemar Pheasant

This recipe uses pheasant breasts. Use the legs for a casserole or stock.
Leeks and bacon go really well in game recipes.

**COOK NOW EAT LATER**

### TO PREPARE AHEAD
Prepare to the end of step 3. Cool quickly, cover and keep in the fridge for up to 1 day. Reheat until piping hot to serve.

### TO FREEZE
It will freeze at the end of step 3 but take care not to overcook the pheasant in the first place. Freeze and thaw completely. Reheat until piping hot, stirring.

### TO COOK IN THE AGA
Cook steps 1 and 2 on the Boiling Plate. At step 3, bring to the boil on the Boiling Plate, cover and transfer to the Simmering Oven for about 10–15 minutes until the pheasant is tender.

100g (4 oz) thickly sliced
  bacon, cut into strips
2 leeks, coarsely shredded
2 tablespoons sunflower oil
6 boneless pheasant breasts,
  skin removed
25g (1 oz) plain flour
300ml (½ pint) apple juice
300ml (½ pint) chicken stock

1 tablespoon cranberry
  or redcurrant jelly
a few sprigs of fresh parsley
1 large sprig of fresh thyme
1 bay leaf
salt and freshly ground
  black pepper
a generous amount of
  chopped fresh parsley

**1** Heat a non-stick frying pan and add the bacon. Cook gently, stirring occasionally, for a few minutes, then add the leeks and cook until the leeks are beginning to brown and the bacon is crisp. Remove the leeks and bacon to a plate.

**2** Heat the oil in the same pan and fry the pheasant breasts quickly on a high heat until browned all over. Lift out and add to the bacon and leeks. Add the flour to the pan and cook, stirring, for 1 minute. Gradually blend in the apple juice, stock and cranberry or redcurrant jelly. Bring to the boil, stirring until thickened.

**3** Return the browned pheasant, bacon and leeks to the pan, and add the parsley sprigs, thyme, bay and seasoning. Bring to the boil, cover and simmer gently for about 10–15 minutes until the pheasant is tender. Keep warm and rest for 15 minutes before serving.

**4** Taste the sauce for seasoning, remove the parsley stalks, thyme and bay leaf, and sprinkle over lots of chopped fresh parsley. Serve with mashed potato.

# Glazed Duck Breasts
## with Blackcurrant Sauce

This is a smart recipe perfect for a dinner party. Quick to make and healthy, too.
Buy a good-quality blackcurrant jam, not too set, more like a conserve.

**COOK NOW
EAT LATER**

**TO PREPARE AHEAD**
The glaze can be made
ahead and spread on
to the duck breasts up
to 8 hours ahead. The
sauce can be made up
to 8 hours ahead.

**TO FREEZE**
Not suitable.

**TO COOK IN THE AGA**
Pan-fry on the Boiling
Plate and roast on the
second set of runners
in the Roasting Oven
for 12 minutes.

2 tablespoons blackcurrant jam
2 teaspoons Worcestershire
 sauce
2 tablespoons olive oil
4 duck breasts
salt and freshly ground
 black pepper

**Sauce**
a knob of butter
1 small onion, finely chopped
150ml (¼ pint) red wine
200ml (7 fl oz) chicken stock
1 teaspoon cornflour

Preheat the oven to 220°C/Fan 200°C /Gas 7.

**1** Measure the blackcurrant jam into a small saucepan.
Gently heat until runny, then leave to cool.

**2** Spoon the cooled jam into a bowl and add the
Worcestershire sauce and oil. Add the duck breasts
and coat them in the mixture. Season well.

**3** Heat a frying pan until hot and brown the duck breasts
for a couple of minutes on each side until golden. (Reserving
the jam and Worcestershire sauce mixture left in the bowl.)
Transfer the duck to a baking sheet and roast in the
preheated oven for 15 minutes. Remove from the oven,
cover with foil and leave to rest for 5 minutes.

**4** Meanwhile, to make the sauce, add the knob of butter
to the used frying pan. Add the onion and fry for a few
minutes until softened. Pour in the wine and boil to
reduce by a third. Add the stock, the blackcurrant jam
and Worcestershire sauce mixture (left in the bowl) and
season with salt and pepper. Measure the cornflour into
a small bowl, add a tablespoon of cold water and mix to a
smooth paste. Add a little of the sauce into the cornflour
bowl to loosen, then stir into the frying pan and boil for
a few minutes. Strain the sauce through a sieve.

**5** Carve the duck breasts into slices and arrange on
a plate. Tip any meat juices into the sauce, stir and
then pour a little sauce over each breast.

# Chicken Olives Provençal

This is a super family supper dish that calls for pitted black olives. Boneless chicken thighs are readily available from all good supermarkets. The stuffing and sauce are very easy to do and the chicken doesn't need browning ahead.

**COOK NOW EAT LATER**

## TO PREPARE AHEAD

Complete to the end of step 3, cover and keep in the fridge for up to 8 hours. Cook as directed in step 4. Or complete to the end of step 4, cool quickly, cover and keep in the fridge for up to 24 hours. Reheat at 200°C/Fan 180°C/Gas 6 for about 20–25 minutes, or until the chicken and sauce are piping hot.

## TO FREEZE

The raw stuffed chicken thighs freeze well. Defrost thoroughly in the fridge overnight before cooking, as from step 4. Or freeze the cooked completed dish. Thaw for 6 hours at room temperature or overnight in the fridge. Reheat as above.

## TO COOK IN THE AGA

For step 4, slide the dish on to the second set of runners in the Roasting Oven for about 25–30 minutes.

3 large good-quality pork
   sausages
25g (1 oz) good-quality pitted
   black olives, finely chopped
finely grated zest of 1 lemon
1 tablespoon finely chopped
   fresh thyme
1 tablespoon finely chopped
   fresh sage
salt and freshly ground
   black pepper
8 chicken thighs, skin
   and bone removed

25g (1 oz) Parmesan,
   coarsely grated
chopped fresh parsley
   to garnish

### Sauce
2 tablespoons dark soy sauce
1 scant tablespoon
   Worcestershire sauce
1 tablespoon runny honey
2 teaspoons grainy mustard
1 × 400g can chopped
   tomatoes

You will need an ovenproof dish about 28 × 23cm (11 × 9 in). Preheat the oven to 190°C/Fan 170°C/Gas 5.

**1** Slit each sausage skin lengthways and remove the meat. Put the sausagemeat into a bowl, add the olives, lemon zest, thyme, sage, salt and pepper, and mix well.

**2** Unfold and lay out the chicken thighs (smooth side down). Season with salt and pepper and fill with a tablespoon of the sausagemeat stuffing (where the bone would have been). Bring each edge of the chicken towards the middle, over the stuffing. Arrange in the dish, join side down. Season the thighs all over.

**3** Blend together the sauce ingredients in a bowl and pour over the thighs, ensuring all are covered. Sprinkle Parmesan over the chicken.

**4** Cook in the preheated oven for about 30–40 minutes until the chicken is tender and the sauce is piping hot.

**5** Garnish with parsley and serve with herby mashed potatoes.

# Thai Fragrant Chicken

There is a wonderful light and subtle flavour to this chicken dish. Ideally, it should be made the day before so that the flavours infuse, and then can be reheated gently to serve. We like a generous amount of sauce but if you like less, reduce the amount of stock. It would then also make a thicker sauce, which you may prefer.

5 large chicken breasts,
    skin and bone removed,
    cut into thin strips
salt and freshly ground
    black pepper
2 tablespoons sunflower oil
1 large onion, finely chopped
2 garlic cloves, crushed
1 × 3cm (1–1½ in) piece
    fresh root ginger, grated
½ teaspoon garam masala
1 × 2.5cm (1 in) piece
    cinnamon stick

seeds of 6 cardamom
    pods, crushed
2 teaspoons ground cumin
1 bay leaf
150ml (¼ pint) chicken stock
1 × 250ml carton coconut
    cream (UHT)
finely grated zest
    and juice of ½–1 lime
chopped fresh coriander

**COOK NOW
EAT LATER**

**TO PREPARE AHEAD**
Make to the end of step
5 the day before. Cool
quickly then store in
the fridge. Reheat
gently until piping
hot, then scatter
with coriander.

**TO FREEZE**
Not suitable.

**1** Season the chicken with salt and pepper. Heat half the oil in a large non-stick pan, add the chicken and quickly brown. Lift out on to a plate. It is best to do this in batches.

**2** Heat the remaining oil in the frying pan, then add the onion, garlic and ginger. Cook for a few minutes over a high heat, then cover and cook gently over a low heat for about 10 minutes until soft.

**3** Add the garam masala, cinnamon, cardamom, cumin and bay leaf, and stir for 1 minute. Add the browned chicken.

*Recipe continued overleaf*

COOK NOW
EAT LATER

**TO COOK IN THE AGA**
Sear the chicken
on the Boiling Plate.
Cook the onion, garlic
and ginger for a few
minutes on the Boiling
Plate, then cover
and transfer to the
Simmering Oven
for about 20 minutes
until soft. Return
to the Boiling Plate
to add the spices,
chicken, stock and
coconut cream. Bring
back to the boil, cover
and transfer to the
Simmering Oven for
about 10 minutes
until cooked.

*Recipe continued*

**4** Blend in the stock and the coconut cream, stirring
continually until it comes to the boil. Season, cover
with the lid and simmer gently for about 5 minutes,
or until the chicken is cooked.

**5** Remove and discard the cinnamon stick and bay
leaf. Stir in the lime zest and juice.

**6** Sprinkle with coriander and serve with Aromatic
Thai Rice (see page 180).

# Chardonnay Chicken
## with Artichoke Hearts

This special chicken casserole goes really well with creamy mashed potato or basmati and wild rice. There is plenty of sauce with this recipe so if you want to give 2 thighs each, or serve more people, add up to 6 more thighs.

8 chicken thighs on the
   bone, skin removed
salt and freshly ground
   black pepper
1 tablespoon olive oil
15g (½ oz) butter
2 large onions, roughly
   chopped
2 garlic cloves, crushed
1 teaspoon caster sugar

25g (1 oz) plain flour
300ml (½ pint) Chardonnay
   or dry white wine
225g (8 oz) small chestnut
   mushrooms, whole
1 × 400g can artichoke hearts
2 tablespoons full-fat
   crème fraîche
4 tablespoons chopped
   fresh parsley

**COOK NOW
EAT LATER**

**1** Season the chicken thighs with salt and pepper. Heat the oil and butter in a large deep frying pan and brown the chicken thighs all over. Lift out on to a plate.

**2** Add the onions, garlic and sugar to the oil remaining in the pan and cook over a low heat for about 15–20 minutes until tender.

**3** Turn up the heat and allow the onions to brown. Sprinkle in the flour, thoroughly blending, add the wine and stir well. Bring to the boil, stirring until thickened.

**4** Return the chicken to the pan with the mushrooms, season and bring to the boil. Simmer over a low heat or transfer to a slow oven at 160°C/Fan 140°C/Gas 3 and cook until the chicken is tender, about 45 minutes.

**5** Drain the artichokes, cut in half and add to the chicken. Heat through gently then add the crème fraîche, check the seasoning and stir in most of the parsley.

**6** Sprinkle with the remaining parsley before serving.

### TO PREPARE AHEAD
Prepare to the end of step 4. Cool quickly, cover and keep in the fridge for up to 24 hours. Reheat until piping hot, stirring in the artichokes towards the end of reheating. Stir in the crème fraîche and parsley to serve.

### TO FREEZE
Cool quickly at the end of step 4 and freeze for 3 months. Thaw overnight in the fridge and reheat until piping hot.

### TO COOK IN THE AGA
Cook the onion at step 2, covered, in the Simmering Oven for 20 minutes. Return to the Boiling Plate for steps 3 and 4. Add the chicken and mushrooms, bring to the boil and cover. Transfer to the Simmering Oven and cook until tender, about 45 minutes. Continue with steps 5 and 6.

# Turkey Salad
## with Avocado, Bacon and Pesto Dressing

Another tasty way to use up the fresh leftover turkey at Christmas, or a lovely summer buffet dish if made with chicken.

**COOK NOW EAT LATER**

**TO PREPARE AHEAD**
Prepare up to the end of step 3. Cover and keep in the fridge up to 24 hours ahead.

**TO FREEZE**
Not suitable.

**TO COOK IN THE AGA**
Fry the bacon on the Boiling Plate the day before and warm in the Simmering Oven for 5 minutes when needed.

175g (6 oz) bacon, cut into small pieces
450g (1 lb) cooked turkey or chicken, free from skin and bone
salt and freshly ground black pepper
50g (2 oz) black olives in olive oil, stoned and cut in half
2 just ripe avocados
3 heaped tablespoons chopped fresh parsley
a small bag of mixed salad leaves

**Dressing**
6 tablespoons olive oil
3 tablespoons balsamic vinegar
1 tablespoon caster sugar
2 tablespoons pesto

**1** Measure the dressing ingredients into a jug and mix together. Season with salt and pepper.

**2** Fry the bacon pieces until crisp and keep warm.

**3** Cut the turkey or chicken into neat pieces, season and toss in two-thirds of the dressing with the olives. This can be left to marinate overnight if you have time.

**4** Peel the avocados, remove the stones, and cut the flesh into large pieces. Gently coat with the remaining dressing and season well.

**5** Just before serving, mix together the turkey or chicken, avocado, parsley and salad leaves. Pile on to a pretty serving dish and sprinkle over the hot bacon.

# Chilean Chicken

A quick and easy dish that looks good enough to serve for a dinner party. There is no sauce to make at the last minute, as the savoury butter can be poured over.

6 chicken breasts, skin
  and bone removed
salt and freshly ground
  black pepper
a few fresh coriander leaves
  to garnish

**Savoury Butter**
125g (4½ oz) butter
2–3 hot red chillies, seeded
3 sun-dried tomatoes in
  oil, drained
1 large garlic clove, peeled
a small bunch of fresh
  coriander

Preheat the oven to 220°C/Fan 200°C/Gas 7.

**1** Place all the savoury butter ingredients, plus some salt and pepper, in a food processor and blend until well mixed and almost smooth.

**2** Beat out the chicken breasts between 2 sheets of clingfilm until thin, using a rolling pin.

**3** Reserve a small amount of the savoury butter. Season the chicken breasts with salt and pepper and spread the butter over them. Roll up tightly lengthways.

**4** Take 6 pieces of foil, big enough to enclose one chicken breast in each. Rub any reserved butter over the foil and put a chicken breast on to each piece. Season again, then fold the foil around the chicken and seal at the side by crimping together.

**5** Put the chicken parcels on to a baking tray and cook in the preheated oven for about 20 minutes, depending on the size of the chicken breasts, until cooked. Allow to rest for a further 10 minutes.

**6** Lift out of the foil, slice the chicken breasts on the diagonal and spoon over the buttery juices. Garnish with coriander and serve with rice.

### TO PREPARE AHEAD

Make the butter up to a week ahead and keep in the fridge. Fill and roll the chicken as in step 3, wrap each one in foil as in step 4 and store in the fridge up to 24 hours ahead. Cook and serve as in steps 5 and 6.

### TO FREEZE

Wrap and freeze the filled, rolled and uncooked chicken for up to 2 months. (NB the chicken must be fresh.) Thaw overnight in the fridge. Continue with steps 5 and 6.

### TO COOK IN THE AGA

Put the foil parcels directly on the Boiling Plate (with the foil join to one side) for 1½–2 minutes to brown the chicken. Turn the whole parcel over into the small roasting tin and transfer to the floor of the Roasting Oven for 12–15 minutes, depending on the size of the chicken breasts.

# Italian Chicken
## with Olives and Tomato

An especially easy supper dish made from store-cupboard ingredients. It reheats well too! You can buy olives stuffed with anchovies, which are ideal for this as the anchovies give saltiness. If you are not keen, just use pitted green olives instead.

**COOK NOW
EAT LATER**

### TO PREPARE AHEAD

Cook completely ahead to the end of step 4, 24 hours ahead. Cool quickly, cover and refrigerate. Reheat carefully, gently stirring, in a pan on the hob until piping hot. Or reheat in the oven preheated to 200°C/Fan 180°C/Gas 6 for about 30 minutes, stirring occasionally. Add a little stock or water if the sauce is too thick.

### TO FREEZE

Freezes well. Cool the cooked chicken quickly and freeze in a container for up to 3 months. Thaw for about 6 hours at room temperature or overnight in the fridge. Reheat as above.

12 chicken thighs, skin removed, bone in
salt and freshly ground black pepper
2–3 tablespoons olive oil
2 large onions, roughly chopped
2 fat garlic cloves, crushed
1 level tablespoon caster sugar
25g (1 oz) plain flour
250ml (9 fl oz) chicken stock, or water and stock cube

1 × 400g can chopped tomatoes
2 teaspoons sun-dried tomato paste
350g (12 oz) olives with anchovies, halved
1 tablespoon balsamic vinegar
3 tablespoons chopped fresh parsley

**1** Season the chicken thighs with salt and pepper.

**2** Heat the oil in a frying pan and fry the onions and garlic for a few minutes. Cover with a lid and cook gently for about 20 minutes until the onions are tender.

**3** Add the sugar to the onions and return to a high heat for a few minutes to lightly brown and caramelise and to drive off any excess liquid. Sprinkle in the flour and mix well. Draw to one side and add the stock and chopped tomatoes, stirring. Return to the heat and bring to the boil. Allow to thicken, adding the sun-dried tomato paste, olives, vinegar and some salt and pepper.

**4** Add the chicken to the pan and bring back to the boil. Cover the pan and cook over a gentle heat for about 20–30 minutes (turning the chicken once), until the chicken is tender. Cut into a thigh with a sharp knife to ensure the juices run clear. If still bloody, continue to cook over a gentle heat until the juices do run clear. Check the seasoning. If the sauce is a bit thick, add a little more stock or water.

**5** Scatter with parsley and serve with basmati and wild rice or tagliatelle and a green salad.

**TO COOK IN THE AGA**
Cook the onions, covered, in the Simmering Oven for about 20 minutes until tender. Use the Boiling Plate for step 3. For step 4, transfer the covered pan to the Roasting Oven for about 10 minutes, and then to the Simmering Oven for a further 10 minutes, or until the chicken is cooked.

# Piquant Chicken with Basil

A delicious family chicken recipe, which will be popular with all ages.
Once you've bought the chicken breasts the rest of the ingredients
are more than likely to be in the store-cupboard.

**COOK NOW
EAT LATER**

## TO PREPARE AHEAD

Cook completely ahead,
to the end of step 3,
cool quickly, cover
and refrigerate for up
to 24 hours. To serve,
cover and reheat in
an oven preheated to
190°C/Fan 170°C/Gas
5 for about 30–40
minutes until piping
hot. Scatter with the
basil to serve.

## TO FREEZE

Cool, pack and freeze
the cooked chicken
without the basil.
Freeze for up to 3
months. Thaw for
about 6 hours at
room temperature
or overnight in the
fridge. Reheat to
serve as above.

## TO COOK IN THE AGA

Cook on the grid shelf
on the floor of the
Roasting Oven for
about 20 minutes,
depending on the size
of the chicken breasts.

2 tablespoons sunflower oil
a good knob of butter
6 chicken breasts,
   skin removed
salt and freshly ground
   black pepper
1 small onion, finely chopped
2 fat garlic cloves, crushed
2 tablespoons cider
   or wine vinegar
1 tablespoon dry mustard
   powder

3 tablespoons light
   muscovado sugar
3–4 tablespoons tomato
   ketchup
3 tablespoons soy sauce
1–2 tablespoons tomato purée
1 × 400g can chopped
   tomatoes
6 sprigs of fresh basil,
   shredded

Preheat the oven to 190°C/Fan 170°C/Gas 5.

**1** Measure the oil and butter into a large non-stick frying
pan and brown the chicken in two batches for 4–5 minutes
on each side. Put in a shallow ovenproof dish and season.

**2** Lower the heat and add the onion and garlic to the pan.
Cover and cook gently until the onion is tender, stirring
occasionally, about 10 minutes. Add the remaining
ingredients, except the basil, to the pan, season and
pour over the chicken.

**3** Cook in the preheated oven for about 20 minutes, until
the chicken is tender. To test that the chicken is cooked
cut into a breast with a sharp knife: the juices from the
chicken should be clear.

**4** Scatter with the fresh basil and serve with pasta and
a mixed green salad.

# Lemon and Thyme Chicken
## with Winter Roasted Vegetables

A one-pot meal. It is essential to cook the vegetables in a wide shallow casserole dish or roasting tin: if the dish is too deep, the vegetables will not take on the crisp, brown, roasted finish. For a heartier dish, use leg or breast joints and cook for about 25 minutes on top of the vegetables.

6 chicken breasts,
   skin removed
juice of 2 lemons
a good bunch of fresh thyme
2 tablespoons olive oil
300ml (½ pint) chicken stock
1 tablespoon cornflour

**Vegetables**
350g (12 oz) peeled
   swede, cubed
275g (10 oz) peeled sweet
   potato, cut into chunks
   (roast potato size)

3 large old potatoes, peeled
   and cut into chunks
   (roast potato size)
225g (8 oz) parsnips, peeled
   and cut in half lengthways
225g (8 oz) medium carrots,
   peeled and cut in half
   lengthways
3 tablespoons olive oil
salt and freshly ground
   black pepper
a few sprigs of fresh thyme
2 medium courgettes,
   cut into thick slices

**COOK NOW EAT LATER**

**TO PREPARE AHEAD**
Marinate the chicken up to 24 hours ahead. Prepare and slightly undercook the vegetables. The night before, brown the chicken as in step 3, cool, cover and keep in the fridge. Continue with steps 4 and 5, cooking for about 20 minutes.

**TO FREEZE**
Not suitable.

**1** Marinate the chicken breasts in the lemon juice, thyme leaves and 1 tablespoon of the olive oil for a few hours, or overnight, if time allows.

Preheat the oven to 200°C/Fan 180°C/Gas 6.

**2** Toss all the vegetables, except the courgettes, in the oil in a large shallow casserole dish or roasting tin, and season with salt and pepper. Add the thyme sprigs. Cook in the preheated oven for about 1½–2 hours, turning occasionally, until the vegetables are cooked and tinged with colour, stirring from time to time. (Do not cover.)

*Recipe continued overleaf*

*Recipe continued*

**3** Lift the chicken breasts from the marinade (reserve the marinade). Heat the remaining oil in a frying pan and brown the chicken breasts on both sides.

**4** About 15 minutes before the vegetables are finished, toss the courgettes in with the vegetables and put the chicken breasts on top of the vegetables in the oven. Return the dish to the oven and cook for a further 15 minutes or so or until the chicken is tender. Remove the thyme sprigs to serve.

**5** Pour the reserved marinade into the frying pan (in which the chicken breasts were browned) and add the chicken stock. Bring to the boil. Slake the cornflour with a little water and add to the pan. Bring to the boil and taste for seasoning. Serve this sauce with the chicken and vegetables.

**TO COOK IN THE AGA**
Cook the vegetables in a roasting tin on the floor of the Roasting Oven for just under 1 hour, stirring halfway through. Brown the breasts on the Boiling Plate. Toss in the courgettes, put the browned chicken breasts on top of the vegetables, and return to the second set of runners in the Roasting Oven for a further 15 minutes or until the vegetables and chicken are tender.

# Chilled Gazpacho Chicken

Gazpacho is an old favourite cold soup for summer. I have combined the raw ingredients with cooked chicken to make an up-to-date Coronation chicken. You can of course use cooked turkey instead of the chicken.

COOK NOW
EAT LATER

## TO PREPARE AHEAD
Prepare the chicken to the end of step 2, cover and keep in the fridge for up to 24 hours ahead. The salad can be prepared up to 12 hours ahead, but do not dress. Spoon the chicken on to a flat serving dish and garnish with the salad and fresh basil.

## TO FREEZE
Not suitable.

## TIP
Peppadew peppers are small bell peppers from South Africa, found in jars in good delis and supermarkets. They are available hot or mild, and we like the mild ones best. Once opened, keep in the fridge, and use them in salads, pasta, stuffed with cream cheese, and in any of the recipes here (see pages 28 and 242).

450g (1 lb) cooked chicken
100ml (3½ fl oz) 'light' low-calorie mayonnaise
100ml (3½ fl oz) full-fat crème fraîche
2 tablespoons sun-dried tomato paste
10 peppadew bell peppers, drained and thinly sliced
1 garlic clove, crushed
6 spring onions, white part only, thinly sliced
2 teaspoons balsamic vinegar
2 tablespoons chopped fresh basil, plus a handful of leaves to garnish
salt and freshly ground black pepper

**Garnish Salad**
1 small cucumber, peeled, seeded and cut into pieces
225g (8 oz) cherry tomatoes, cut in half
50g (2 oz) black olives (the best are in olive oil from the deli counter)
chopped fresh parsley
a little French dressing

**1** Cut the chicken into neat bite-sized pieces, removing all the skin and bone.

**2** Mix the mayonnaise and crème fraîche with the tomato paste, peppers and garlic. Fold in the chicken pieces and spring onions, then taste and season carefully with the balsamic vinegar, basil, salt and pepper.

**3** Spoon out on to a flat serving dish and garnish with the dressed salad and basil leaves.

# Oriental Chicken Stir-fry

SERVES 6

Sweet chilli sauce can be bought in a bottle and gives a great flavour and glaze to the chicken.

**COOK NOW EAT LATER**

**TO PREPARE AHEAD**
The chicken can be marinated in the sweet chilli sauce up to a day ahead. Prepare all the ingredients up to 4 hours ahead ready to cook.

**TO FREEZE**
Not suitable.

**TO COOK IN THE AGA**
Cook on the Boiling Plate.

2 tablespoons sweet chilli sauce
500g (1 lb 2 oz) chicken breast, boneless, skinless, sliced into strips
salt and freshly ground black pepper
3 tablespoons sunflower oil
1 red pepper, seeded and cubed
3 medium carrots, peeled, halved lengthways and sliced very thinly on the diagonal
1 tablespoon fresh ginger, finely grated

1 garlic clove, crushed
150g (5 oz) baby corn, sliced into three on the diagonal
200g (7 oz) small chestnut mushrooms, halved
200g (7 oz) sugar snap peas

**Sauce**
2 tablespoons sweet chilli sauce
2 tablespoons dark soy sauce
1 tablespoon cornflour
200ml (7 fl oz) chicken stock

**1** Measure 2 tablespoons of chilli sauce into a bowl and stir in the chicken strips. Season well. Heat a large frying pan until hot. Add 1 tablespoon of the oil, add the chicken and fry over a high heat until golden brown and just cooked through. Transfer to a plate.

**2** To make the sauce, measure the sweet chilli sauce, soy and cornflour into a bowl and stir until smooth. Blend in the stock and season with salt and pepper.

**3** Heat the remaining oil in the frying pan. Add the red pepper and carrots and stir-fry for 3–4 minutes. Add the ginger, garlic and remaining vegetables and fry for another 3–4 minutes until just cooked.

**4** Add the chicken and sauce and toss together for 2 minutes. Check the seasoning and serve with rice or egg noodles.

COOK NOW, EAT LATER

✦

# Meat

## CHAPTER FOUR

Meat stews and casseroles can, like poultry dishes, be completely cooked ahead and chilled for a day or so, or frozen. They should be cooked until tender but never overcooked, or the meat chunks could fall apart when reheated. Again, as with chicken, tasting is vital, especially when cooking ahead. Taste, then adjust the seasoning as appropriate, but not just with salt and pepper. If something has a lot of tomatoes in it, you may need a pinch of sugar. Perhaps some lemon juice or redcurrant jelly may be needed.

It's not a fallacy that some meat and poultry dishes just do taste better when reheated. The flavours, especially of spicy dishes and those containing red wine, have time to mature and come together. And even with dishes that cannot be fully prepared ahead, some flavour advantages can be gained: a stuffing can flavour raw meat during an overnight chilling, and a marinade can add flavour and tenderise at the same time.

Ordering the meat in advance from your butcher will also save you time. You can store prime cuts in the fridge for a few days. (Remove the butcher's plastic and rewrap in greaseproof or non-stick parchment paper.)

# Pork Escalopes
## with Apple and Onion

A very easy supper dish, but also good for a dinner party. I use wooden skewers and soak them first to prevent them burning.

**COOK NOW EAT LATER**

### TO PREPARE AHEAD

Brown the stuffed pork and slightly *under*cook 24 hours ahead. Reheat, covered, in an oven preheated to 200°C/ Fan 180°C/Gas 6 for about 8 minutes to serve. The sauce can be made completely and sieved ahead.

### TO FREEZE

Not suitable.

### TO COOK IN THE AGA

Cook the onion and apple stuffing, covered, in the Simmering Oven for about 15–20 minutes, until tender. Brown the pork ahead on the Boiling Plate and reheat, covered, on the second set of runners in the Roasting Oven for about 6–8 minutes until hot. Reheat the sauce gently on the Simmering Plate.

6 × 225g (8 oz) lean pork chops
a knob of butter
1 small onion, finely chopped
1 large cooking apple, peeled, cored and coarsely grated
1 tablespoon chopped fresh parsley
1 tablespoon chopped fresh thyme
finely grated zest of 1 lemon

salt and freshly ground black pepper
about 1 tablespoon sunflower oil

**Sauce**
150ml (¼ pint) apple juice
1 teaspoon light muscovado sugar
150ml (¼ pint) double cream

**1** Remove the bone and some of the fat from the chops and slit horizontally through the meat from the bone side. Do not cut right through but leave an open pocket.

**2** Heat a little butter in a frying pan and sauté the onion for a few minutes. Add the apple and gently soften for about 15 minutes. When the onion is tender, add the herbs, lemon zest and seasoning. Allow to cool.

**3** Fill each chop with the stuffing and secure with a wooden skewer. Season.

**4** Heat a little oil in a large frying pan and fry the chops over a high heat for 3–4 minutes on each side. Turn the heat down and cook for a further 6–7 minutes. Transfer to a plate, cover while making the sauce, allowing the meat to rest. Keep warm.

**5** Deglaze the pan with the apple juice and reduce over a high heat to about 3 tablespoons. Add the sugar and cream and boil for a couple of minutes. Season to taste. Sieve the sauce and serve with the pork chops.

**SERVES 12**

# Mango-glazed Gammon
## with Mango and Mint Salsa

Ham is always a top favourite, whether served hot or cold. If cooking ham near Christmas time, the ham skin is excellent placed over the turkey breast for roasting to keep the breast moist. Gammon is raw cured bacon leg, and it is called ham when it is cooked. This needs so little preparation, it is the fastest cut-and-come-again meat to do for a crowd.

**COOK NOW
EAT LATER**

**TO PREPARE AHEAD**
You can cook and brown the gammon 1–2 days ahead, then cool and chill it. Don't carve too soon, though, or the gammon will lose its pink colour.

**TO FREEZE**
Not suitable.

**TO COOK IN THE AGA**
Arrange the gammon snugly in a large pan. Cover with fruit juice as above. Bring to the boil on the Boiling Plate, cover and transfer to the Simmering Oven to cook. It will take 2–3 hours until it is tender. Brown towards the top of the Roasting Oven for about 15 minutes, turning round once.

1 × 2.6kg (6 lb) gammon
1 × 1-litre (1¾ pint) carton orange and mango juice or tropical fruit juice
mango chutney to glaze
a few cloves

**Salsa**
about 4 tablespoons mango chutney
1 large mango, peeled and neatly chopped
1 small fresh red chilli, seeded and finely chopped
2.5cm (1 in) piece fresh root ginger, peeled and grated
4 tablespoons chopped fresh mint
1 tablespoon white wine vinegar
finely grated rind and juice of 1 lime

**1** Weigh the joint and calculate the cooking time. Allow 20 minutes per 450g (1 lb) and 20 minutes over.

**2** Put the joint in a saucepan just big enough to take it, and cover with the fruit juice and a lid. (Add some water if not covered completely.) Bring to the boil over a high heat, turn the heat down and simmer very gently for the calculated time.

**3** About 15 minutes before the end of the cooking time, preheat the grill to its highest setting.

**4** Remove the gammon from the juice (reserve the juice). Leave to cool slightly. Cut off any string, and peel off the skin. Spread mango chutney thickly over the fatty surface. Score the fat to make a lattice pattern and stud with a few cloves.

**5** Cover the lean meat around the sides with foil and put the gammon in a grill pan lined with foil. Pour some of the reserved juice inside the foil and slide the gammon under the preheated grill to cook until golden brown and an even colour.

**6** For the salsa, simply mix all the ingredients together and serve with the hot or cold gammon.

**TIP**
Check with your butcher when you buy your gammon whether or not it needs to be soaked before cooking to remove the saltiness. Supermarket gammon usually does not need soaking as the cure is milder.

# Thai Pork Curry

Traditionally Thai dishes do not contain flour, but I think it gives the sauce a more stable consistency. If you prefer, use chicken, a small breast each, or prawns.

## TO PREPARE AHEAD

Complete to the end of step 4. Cool quickly, cover and keep in the fridge for up to 24 hours. Reheat until piping hot, adding the lime and parsley or coriander to serve.

## TO FREEZE

Cool quickly and freeze at the end of step 4, omitting the water chestnuts. Thaw overnight in the fridge, add the water chestnuts and reheat until piping hot. Expect the sauce to separate on thawing. It will come together once reheated in a pan, stirring.

## TO COOK IN THE AGA

Cook the onions, covered, in the Simmering Oven for about 20–30 minutes until tender. Brown the pork on the Boiling Plate, then continue with the rest of the steps.

700g (1 ½ lb) pork fillet, cut into fine strips
2–3 tablespoons red Thai curry paste
2 tablespoons sunflower oil
2 large onions, thinly sliced
1 level tablespoon plain flour
1 × 400ml can coconut milk
2 tablespoons Thai fish sauce
1 tablespoon granulated sugar
1 × 220g can water chestnuts, drained and halved
juice and finely grated zest of ½ lime
chopped fresh parsley or coriander
salt and freshly ground black pepper

**1** Marinate the pork in 1 tablespoon of the curry paste for 30 minutes.

**2** Heat the oil in a large frying pan, add the onions and cook gently for about 10 minutes until they are tender. Lift the onions out on to a plate.

**3** Increase the heat and brown the pork. This will probably have to be done in 2 batches.

**4** Remove the pork from the pan and return the onions with 1–2 tablespoons red Thai curry paste and the flour. Stirring well, add the coconut milk, fish sauce, sugar, water chestnuts and pork. Bring to the boil, cover and cook gently for about 5 minutes, until the pork and sauce are just boiling.

**5** Just before serving add the lime juice and zest and lots of parsley or coriander. Taste for seasoning. Serve with rice.

SERVES 6

# Roast Pork Fillets
## with Apple and Fennel Sauce

An all in one dish – inspired by one of our Aga ladies!

50g (2 oz) butter
2 × 225g (8 oz) fennel bulbs,
   trimmed and finely diced
2 large cooking apples, peeled,
   cored and finely diced
salt and freshly ground
   black pepper
2 × 500g (1 lb 2 oz) pork
   fillets/tenderloins, trimmed
fresh sage leaves to garnish

**Stuffing**
175g (6 oz) onions, chopped
150ml (¼ pint) water
40g (1 ½ oz) butter
100g (4 oz) soft white
   breadcrumbs
½ teaspoon dried sage

**TO PREPARE AHEAD**
Make the stuffing
up to 24 hours ahead.
Stuff the pork up to
24 hours ahead, cover
and refrigerate until
ready to cook.

**TO FREEZE**
Not suitable.

**TO COOK IN THE AGA**
Cook the stuffing
on the Boiling Plate.
Roast the stuffed fillets
on the grid shelf on the
floor of the Roasting
Oven for 30 minutes
or until tender.

Preheat the oven to 220°C/Fan 200°C/Gas 7.

**1** First prepare the stuffing. Put the onions and
water together in a pan and bring to the boil. Cook for
10 minutes or until the onions are just tender but not
soft. Drain and return the onions to the hot pan with
the butter. Once the butter has melted, stir in the
remaining stuffing ingredients, seasoning generously
with salt and pepper. Allow to cool.

**2** For the pork, melt the butter in a pan, add the fennel
and apples and cook until almost soft. Season well with
salt and pepper then spoon into the base of a medium
roasting tin.

**3** Cut the pork fillets about halfway through lengthways,
and spread out into a broad 'V'. Spoon the stuffing into
the 'V' and place on top of the bed of fennel and apple.

**4** Cook in the preheated oven for 30–35 minutes until
the pork is tender and the stuffing crispy and brown.
Lift the pork out of the tin and keep warm.

**5** Mash down the apple and fennel in the roasting tin
to make a sauce. Slice the pork, garnish with sage
leaves and serve with the apple and fennel sauce.

# Baked Sausages
## with Double Onion Marmalade

This method of cooking sausages keeps them wonderfully succulent.

**COOK NOW EAT LATER**

### TO PREPARE AHEAD

Cook to end of step 4. Cool, cover and store in the fridge for up to 2 days. To reheat, cover and cook in an oven preheated to 190°C/ Fan 170°C/Gas 5 for about 30–40 minutes or until piping hot. Scatter with parsley to serve.

### TO FREEZE

Cook to the end of step 4. Cool and freeze for up to 3 months. Thaw overnight in the fridge. Reheat as above.

### TO COOK IN THE AGA

Brown the sausages on the floor of the Roasting Oven, turning them occasionally. Cook the onions, covered, in the Simmering Oven for about 30 minutes. Transfer the onions and sausages to an ovenproof dish, and put on the grid shelf on the floor of the Roasting Oven for about 45 minutes.

about 1 tablespoon sunflower oil
about 25g (1 oz) butter
900g (2 lb) good-quality sausages
450g (1 lb) red onions, thinly sliced
2 large white onions, about 450g (2 lb) in weight, thinly sliced

225ml (8 fl oz) red wine
50ml (2 fl oz) red or white wine vinegar
2 tablespoons caster sugar
salt and freshly ground black pepper
about 3 tablespoons chopped fresh parsley

Preheat the oven to 200°C/Fan 180°C/Gas 6.

**1** Heat the oil and butter over a high heat in a large frying pan and brown the sausages evenly. You will need to do this in 2 batches. Lift the sausages out and drain on kitchen paper.

**2** Pour off excess fat so that about 2 tablespoons remain in the pan. Add the onions to the pan and cook gently, stirring occasionally, for 10–15 minutes or until soft.

**3** Add the wine, vinegar, sugar and seasoning to the onions. Bring to the boil and allow to bubble for a couple of minutes. Transfer to an ovenproof dish.

**4** Arrange the sausages in a single layer on top of the onions and cook, uncovered, in the preheated oven for about 45 minutes. Stir the onions occasionally: they should be soft.

**5** Scatter with lots of parsley and serve with mashed potato (see page 183).

# Penne Pasta with Parma Ham

SERVES 6

A wonderful pasta recipe. Serve with chunks of fresh bread and fresh green salad leaves. Dry-cured ham usually comes in packets of between 70g and 100g. Asparagus tips are the short, thin asparagus spears sold in supermarkets but not usually available in greengrocers.

**COOK NOW EAT LATER**

## TO PREPARE AHEAD

Cook the pasta up to 6 hours ahead, adding the asparagus for the last 3 minutes. Drain the pasta, leave in the colander, refresh in cold water, drain again and cover with clingfilm. Fry the ham until crisp and leave in the pan. About 5 minutes before serving, re-crisp the ham for a moment, remove half and keep warm. Continue as from step 3.

## TO FREEZE

Not suitable.

## TO COOK IN THE AGA

Cook the pasta and ham on the Boiling Plate. Keep half of the ham warm in the Simmering Oven. Finish on the Boiling Plate.

500g (1 lb 2 oz) dried penne pasta
salt and freshly ground black pepper
225g (8 oz) asparagus tips
150g (5 oz) Serrano, Parma or Black Forest ham, snipped into pieces
450g (1 lb) small chestnut mushrooms, sliced
1 × 400ml carton full-fat crème fraîche
about 50g (2 oz) Parmesan, freshly grated
a good handful of chopped fresh parsley

**1** Cook the pasta in a large pan of boiling salted water over a high heat, as directed on the packet, until al dente. Some 3 minutes before the end of cooking, add the asparagus tips. Drain and refresh in cold water, then set aside to drain.

**2** Fry the ham in a large, non-stick frying pan until crisp. Remove half of the ham and keep warm.

**3** Add the mushrooms to the pan and stir with the ham for a moment, then mix in the crème fraîche and half the Parmesan. Season with a little salt and pepper (go easy on the salt as the ham is salty), and bring to the boil.

**4** Return the cooked pasta and asparagus to the first large pan, and add the contents of the frying pan (ham and crème fraîche). Stir well until piping hot and check the seasoning.

**5** Sprinkle over the remaining Parmesan, reserved ham and the parsley. Serve at once.

# Calf's Liver
## with Caramelised Onions and Balsamic Gravy

You can of course fry the onions, but caramelising them in the oven is a bit different! If you can't get calf's liver, use lamb's instead.

700g (1½ lb) calf's liver, thinly
  sliced (trimmed weight)
plain flour
salt and freshly ground
  black pepper
40g (1½ oz) butter

**Caramelised Onions**
3 large mild onions
olive oil
a little granulated sugar

**Gravy**
20g (¾ oz) butter
20g (¾ oz) plain flour
450ml (¾ pint) beef stock
1½ teaspoons soy sauce
1½ dessertspoons
  balsamic vinegar
a little gravy browning
  (optional)

**COOK NOW
EAT LATER**

**TO PREPARE AHEAD**
Earlier in the day,
brown the liver very
quickly until golden,
about 30 seconds to
1 minute on each side.
Lift out, cool, cover and
keep in the fridge until
needed. Cook the onions
in the oven. Set aside.
When ready to serve,
reheat the liver and
the onions in the oven
preheated to 220°C/
Fan 200°C/Gas 7, for
about 10 minutes
depending upon the
thickness of the liver.

**TO FREEZE**
Not suitable.

**TO COOK IN THE AGA**
Cook the onions on a
baking sheet on the
floor of the Roasting
Oven for 20–25
minutes, turning
halfway through.
Brown the liver quickly
on the Boiling Plate.

Preheat the oven to 220°C/Fan 200°C/Gas 7.

**1** Peel and thickly slice the onions into rounds 1cm (½ in) thick. Arrange on a well-greased baking sheet. Brush the onion slices with olive oil and a little sugar to caramelise. Cook in the preheated oven for about 30 minutes, turning and seasoning halfway through.

**2** Toss the liver in seasoned flour. Heat a non-stick frying pan until very hot then add the butter. Add the liver and cook over a high heat for 1–2 minutes on each side until browned all over and just done in the middle – i.e. no longer showing blood when cut. You may have to do this in two batches. Lift out the liver and keep warm.

**3** To make the gravy, melt the butter in a small pan, blend in the flour, then add the stock and bring to the boil. Add the soy sauce, balsamic vinegar and some salt and pepper. Add a dash of gravy browning, if liked, and check the seasoning.

**4** Serve the liver with the caramelised onion rings, balsamic gravy and creamy mashed potatoes.

# Pork, Leek and Sage Burgers

These make a lovely change from classic beef burgers
and are nice served in a bun with apple sauce.

2 small leeks, trimmed
and finely chopped
500g (1 lb 2 oz) minced
pork (not too lean)
75g (3 oz) fresh white
breadcrumbs
2–3 teaspoons whole
grain mustard

salt and freshly ground
black pepper
40g (1 ½ oz) Parmesan,
freshly grated
1 tablespoon finely
chopped fresh sage
2 tablespoons olive oil

**TO PREPARE AHEAD**
Burgers can be made
up to 2 days ahead
and kept in the fridge.

**TO FREEZE**
Burgers can be frozen
raw and kept for up to
3 months.

**TO COOK IN THE AGA**
Fry on the Boiling Plate.

**1** Bring a pan of salted water to the boil, add the leeks
and boil for 4 minutes until just tender. Drain and
refresh in cold water. Press the leeks between two
pieces of kitchen paper to remove any excess water.

**2** Place the mince, breadcrumbs and mustard in a
processor, season with salt and pepper and whiz for
a few minutes until combined. Tip into a mixing bowl.

**3** Add the leeks, Parmesan and sage and mix with
your hands until combined.

**4** Divide into eight and shape into even-sized burgers.
Chill to firm a little before cooking.

**5** Place a non-stick frying pan on a high heat, add
the oil and fry the burgers for about 6 minutes or
so on each side, until golden and cooked through.

**6** Serve with a salad and some apple sauce.

# Marinated Roast Lamb
## with Minted Couscous and Whisky Gravy

SERVES 6

The minted couscous is roasted with the lamb. You may need to cover it with foil to stop it getting too brown or, if preferred, roast it in a separate buttered dish. Use a meat thermometer to obtain the perfect roast.

**COOK NOW
EAT LATER**

### TO PREPARE AHEAD
Marinate the lamb overnight in the fridge. The couscous can be prepared as in the beginning of step 2, and the bowl put in the fridge overnight. Transfer to the buttered dish and cook as from step 3.

### TO FREEZE
Not suitable.

### TO COOK IN THE AGA
At step 3, slide the dish on to the second set of runners in the Roasting Oven for about 1 hour. You may need to cover the couscous with foil. Allow to rest, covered, for 15 minutes in the Simmering Oven.

1.5kg (3¼ lb) leg of lamb (before boning), main leg bone removed to the ball and socket
1 tablespoon cornflour
350ml (12 fl oz) water
chopped parsley to garnish

**Marinade**
7 tablespoons soy sauce
50g (2 oz) light muscovado sugar
4 tablespoons whisky
juice of ½ lemon
1 tablespoon Worcestershire sauce

**Roasted Couscous**
350g (12 oz) couscous
600ml (1 pint) stock, or stock cube and water
275g (10 oz) ready-to-eat dried apricots, snipped into pieces
4 generous tablespoons bottled mint sauce
4 fat garlic cloves, crushed
salt and freshly ground black pepper

Preheat the oven to 220°C/Fan 200°C/Gas 7. Butter an oblong, ovenproof dish, about 28 × 33 × 5cm (11 × 13 × 2 in), large enough to hold the couscous and lamb.

**1** Measure the marinade ingredients into a strong polythene bag, add the lamb to the bag and seal the top. Put in the fridge overnight. Drain off the marinade liquid the next day and reserve.

**2** Measure the couscous into a bowl, pour on the boiling stock, add the other ingredients and season well with salt and pepper. Spoon all the couscous into the buttered dish, leaving space for the lamb. (At this stage the couscous is slightly sloppy: as it cooks, it firms up.)

**3** Transfer the lamb to the dish, placing it upside down. Insert a meat thermometer and roast in the preheated oven for about 30 minutes. Turn the lamb over after this time, and stir the couscous, covering the couscous with foil if it is getting too brown. Reduce the oven temperature to 200°C/Fan 180°C/Gas 6 and cook for a further 1–1½ hours until the temperature on the thermometer reads about 75°C for medium lamb. Remove from the oven and rest, covered, for 15 minutes whilst making the gravy.

**4** For the gravy, mix the cornflour, marinade and water together in a small pan and whisk over a high heat until thickened. Adjust the seasoning. Carve the meat and put alongside the couscous in the dish. Scatter with parsley to serve.

**TIP**
Meat thermometers are wonderful. I use the one on a spike with a spinning dial (I trust it more than a digital one!). You can add it at the beginning or at the end of cooking but ensure it's inserted into the thickest part of the meat, not touching any bone. To be sure the thermometer is working, put the spike into boiling water and check the temperature.

# Tagine of Lamb

**SERVES 6–8**

A traditional Moroccan dish, which is best made a day ahead and reheated.

## COOK NOW EAT LATER

### TO PREPARE AHEAD

Complete to the end of step 3 a day ahead. Cool quickly, cover and keep in the fridge. Reheat on a low heat on the hob until piping hot.

### TO FREEZE

Cool quickly at the end of step 3. Pack into a freezer-proof container and freeze for up to 3 months. Thaw overnight in the fridge. Reheat as above until piping hot.

### TO COOK IN THE AGA

Sear the lamb on the Boiling Plate. Cook the onions covered in the Simmering Oven for 20 minutes. Cook the lamb to the end of step 3 in the Simmering Oven. Check from time to time, returning to the Boiling Plate if it is not cooking. Test if the meat is tender after about 2 hours, depending on the temperature of your Simmering Oven.

1 tablespoon sunflower oil
900g (2 lb) neck fillet of lamb or lean boneless leg or shoulder of lamb, cut into 2.5cm (1 in) pieces
2 large onions, coarsely chopped
3 fat garlic cloves, crushed
175g (6 oz) ready-to-eat dried apricots, quartered
1 teaspoon ground ginger
1 teaspoon ground cinnamon
1 tablespoon paprika
⅛ teaspoon hot chilli powder
a generous pinch of saffron, soaked in 3 tablespoons hot water
2 tablespoons honey
2 × 400g cans chopped tomatoes
salt and freshly ground black pepper
chopped parsley and mint to garnish

Preheat the oven to 160°C/Fan 140°C/Gas 3.

**1** Heat the oil in a large frying pan and brown the lamb in batches. When brown remove with a slotted spoon and put on a plate to one side.

**2** Add the onions and garlic to the pan, stir then cover and cook over a gentle heat for about 10–15 minutes until soft.

**3** Increase the heat and add the apricots, spices, including the saffron and soaking liquid, honey, tomatoes and browned lamb to the pan. Bring to the boil, season, cover and cook in the preheated oven for about 2 hours until the meat is very tender. Check the seasoning.

**4** Garnish with parsley and mint and serve with couscous.

# Roast Short Saddle of Lamb
## with Rosemary and Redcurrant Gravy

A saddle of lamb is both joints cut between the best end of neck and the leg. It also includes the kidneys and tail which are tied and skewered to the joint in a decorative fashion, ready for roasting. Ask your butcher to bone the joint (for easy carving) but then to tie it back on the bone in its original position so that the joint will retain maximum flavour. For carving, simply untie the string. It is a good idea to order the saddle well ahead.

**COOK NOW EAT LATER**

### TO PREPARE AHEAD
Order the meat from the butcher well ahead. Keep in the fridge for up to 2 days prior to roasting. Make the gravy base the day before.

### TO FREEZE
Not suitable.

### TO COOK IN THE AGA
Roast in the Roasting Oven with the roasting tin on the lowest set of runners, for slightly shorter times than the conventional oven, i.e. 10 minutes per 450g (1 lb).

1.75kg (3½ lb) short saddle of lamb, skinned, boned, excess fat removed and reassembled (see above)
salt and freshly ground black pepper
butter for greasing
1 tablespoon redcurrant jelly
1 garlic clove, cut into slivers
1 sprig of fresh rosemary, plus extra for garnish

**Gravy**
2 tablespoons sunflower oil
a knob of butter
1 large onion, roughly chopped
1 sprig of fresh rosemary
1 heaped tablespoon plain flour
450ml (¾ pint) stock
150ml (¼ pint) red wine
1 tablespoon redcurrant jelly
1 teaspoon lemon juice
1 teaspoon Worcestershire sauce
a little gravy browning (optional)

Preheat the oven to 200°C/Fan 180°C/Gas 6.

**1** First make the gravy base which can be made well ahead. Heat the oil and butter in a wide-based pan, add the onion and rosemary, and fry for a few minutes. Stir in the flour, and cook for a few more minutes. Pour on the stock and wine, stirring continually until smooth, and bring to the boil. Season with salt, pepper, redcurrant jelly, lemon juice and Worcestershire sauce. Just before carving tip the pan juices into the gravy and strain out the onion and rosemary. Add a little gravy browning to colour if necessary.

**2** Line a large roasting tin with foil, season the lamb all over and sit the meat in the roasting tin. Cover the kidneys with buttered foil (this way they won't overcook). Spread the redcurrant jelly over the saddle. Tuck some of the garlic and rosemary under the lamb and the remainder around the sides of the meat.

**3** Roast in the preheated oven for 15 minutes per 450g (1 lb) for medium lamb. Check after 20 minutes to see how the saddle is browning. When a perfect rich brown, cover loosely with foil. Turn the tin around halfway through the cooking time. Allow the lamb to rest for 45 minutes and up to 1 hour, still leaving it in the roasting tin covered with foil in an oven at 140°C/Fan 120°C/Gas 1 (If you have no oven space take it from the very hot oven and at once cover and wrap the tin with a thick towel.)

**4** To serve, cut in half lengthways down the back, then thickly slice on the diagonal. This I find best, though the more old-fashioned way is to carve strips parallel to the back bone down the full length of the meat.

**5** Garnish with rosemary and serve with the gravy, mint sauce and redcurrant jelly.

**TIP**
The raw meat will also be improved if left maturing in the fridge for up to 2 days – it will have a better flavour. The resting time after roasting is very important as well (see recipe).

# Lancashire Lamb Shanks

It is wonderful that we can buy lamb shanks so easily in supermarkets. They are often cooked with a tomato and red wine sauce, so I have developed this recipe using a light sauce with white wine and herbs. Do cook the shanks really well until the meat falls off the bone. If you like crisper vegetables, add them to the stew for the last hour only.

6 lamb shanks, about 350g (12 oz) each in weight
salt and freshly ground black pepper
½ tablespoon sunflower oil
50g (2 oz) butter
75g (3 oz) plain flour
600ml (1 pint) white wine
450ml (¾ pint) good chicken or lamb stock
1 large onion, peeled and cut into eighths
1 large carrot, peeled, cut into 2.5cm (1 in) batons
1 butternut squash, total weight 450g (1 lb), peeled and cut into 2.5cm (1 in) slices
masses of chopped fresh parsley

**COOK NOW EAT LATER**

1 Heat a large frying pan. Season the lamb shanks with salt and pepper. Brown the shanks in the oil and butter on each side until golden brown (you will need to do this in batches). Transfer the shanks to a deep casserole dish, large enough to hold all 6 of them (and the vegetables).

2 Add the flour to the fat left in the original pan and mix together off the heat. Return to the heat and gradually add the wine and stock. Bring to the boil, stirring all the time, until the sauce boils and becomes thickish and smooth in consistency. Season with salt and pepper and pour this sauce over the shanks in the casserole.

3 Bring the sauce and shanks back to the boil, cover with a lid and simmer for about 1 hour.

4 Add the vegetables, pushing them down so they are covered with the sauce, and bring back to the boil. Cover with the lid and simmer for a further 1–1½ hours or until the vegetables are tender and the meat is falling off the bone. Check the seasoning. (If preferred, cook in a preheated oven at 160°C/Fan 140°C/Gas 3, following instructions as above.)

5 Stir in the parsley and serve with leeks and mash.

**TO PREPARE AHEAD**
The whole casserole can be made up to 2 days before and kept covered in the fridge. Add the vegetables for slightly less time, as they will continue to cook when the casserole is reheated. Reheat gently, so as not to break up the vegetables, on a low heat on the hob until piping hot.

**TO FREEZE**
Not suitable.

**TO COOK IN THE AGA**
Brown the shanks on the Boiling Plate until golden brown. Cook from step 3 covered in the Simmering Oven for about 2–2½ hours or until the shanks are tender.

# Pan-fried Fillet Steaks
## with Fresh Herb Sauce

It is difficult to make a small quantity of hollandaise sauce, unless you have
a small herb processor. I have given instructions to make the hollandaise
by hand – it really is quite easy!

**COOK NOW
EAT LATER**

### TO PREPARE AHEAD

For steaks, complete
step 3, cool at once,
and put on a buttered
baking sheet. When
cold, cover and keep
in the fridge for up to
12 hours ahead. When
ready to serve, reheat
in a preheated oven at
220°C/Fan 200°C/Gas 7
for about 7–10 minutes
until very hot. Make
the fresh herb sauce on
the day. Don't attempt
to keep hot, leave at
room temperature.

### TO FREEZE

Not suitable.

### TO COOK IN THE AGA

Fry the steaks on the
Boiling Plate. Reheat
the steaks on the
second set of runners
in the Roasting Oven
for about 7 minutes.

6 × 175g (6 oz) thick fillet
  steaks
salt and freshly ground
  black pepper
a little butter
1–2 tablespoons olive oil

**Hollandaise/Herb Sauce**
2 tablespoons lemon juice
225g (8 oz) unsalted butter
4 egg yolks
1 tablespoon each of chopped
  fresh parsley, marjoram
  and chives

**1** To make the sauce, strain the lemon juice into a hot
2.2 litre (4 pint) heatproof mixing bowl. (Heat the bowl
by pouring in water from the kettle just off the boil.)
Melt the butter until bubbling in a small pan.

**2** Add the egg yolks to the lemon juice and add some
salt and pepper. Pour the hot butter slowly on to the egg
yolks, in a steady stream, whisking continuously with a
balloon whisk, or electric hand beater. The sauce should
just hold its shape. Stir the herbs into the sauce and
adjust the seasoning.

**3** To cook the steaks, season them on both sides with salt
and pepper. Spread one side of each with butter. Heat a
large ridged grill pan or frying pan until very hot and add
the oil. Add the steaks, buttered side down, and cook over
a high heat for 2 minutes on each side for medium rare.
Lower the heat and continue to cook until the steaks are
to your liking (an extra 3 minutes on each side for well-
done steaks).

**4** Serve each steak with the fresh herb sauce, which
melts over the hot steak.

# Steak and Mushroom Pie
## with Dauphinoise Potato Topping

SERVES 6

It is important to part-cook the potatoes ahead, otherwise they will go black.

**COOK NOW EAT LATER**

### TO PREPARE AHEAD

Prepare and cook the steak to the end of step 3. Cool, cover and keep in the fridge for up to 2 days. Cook, slice and toss the potatoes in the melted butter earlier in the day. Assemble the pie as step 5, and cook as step 6, allowing a little longer from cold.

### TO FREEZE

Freeze the cooked meat for up to 3 months. Thaw overnight, then assemble the pie, and reheat as above, allowing a little longer from cold.

### TO COOK IN THE AGA

Fry the onions and meat and make the gravy on the Boiling Plate. Transfer to the Simmering Oven, covered, for about 2–3 hours or until tender. Continue with steps 4 and 5. When the topping is added, cook at the top of the Roasting Oven for 30 minutes until golden brown.

1kg (2¼ lb) stewing steak, cut into 2.5cm (1 in) cubes
sunflower oil
2 large onions, roughly chopped
350g (12 oz) small open (dark-gilled) mushrooms, sliced
a good 2 tablespoons plain flour
about 600ml (1 pint) beef stock
1 tablespoon Worcestershire sauce

salt and freshly ground black pepper
a little gravy browning (optional)

**Dauphinoise Potato Topping**
1.1kg (2½ lb) potatoes, peeled
about 50g (2 oz) butter, melted
50g (2 oz) Cheddar, grated

You will need a shallow ovenproof dish, about 30 × 23 × 6cm (12 × 9 × 2½ in).

**1** Brown the meat, in batches, in a little oil in a large frying pan, over a high heat. Remove from the pan.

**2** Add the onion to the pan, fry for a couple of minutes, then lower the heat and simmer for about 10 minutes until soft. Add the mushrooms and flour. Cook, stirring, for 1 minute then add the stock, Worcestershire sauce, seasoning and a little gravy browning, if liked. Bring to the boil and allow to thicken, stirring until smooth.

**3** Return the meat to the pan, bring back to the boil, then cover and simmer very gently for about 2 hours, until the meat is tender. (Or cook in the oven preheated to 160°C/Fan 140°C/Gas 3 until tender.)

**4** For the topping, cook the potatoes in boiling salted water until just tender. Cool a little, slice thickly and toss in the melted butter.

Preheat the oven to 200°C/Fan 180°C/Gas 6.

**5** Spoon the meat into the ovenproof dish. Layer the potatoes on top, seasoning well in between the layers. Top with the cheese.

**6** Cook in the preheated oven for about 30 minutes until the cheese is bubbling and golden and the meat is hot through.

# Venison and Beef
## with Port and Apricots

Casserole venison, ready cubed, can be found in many major supermarkets.
Otherwise, use the meat from the shoulder or haunch.

**COOK NOW
EAT LATER**

## TO PREPARE AHEAD

Cook the casserole
ahead (omitting the
parsley), cool quickly,
cover and keep in the
fridge for up to 2 days.
Reheat until piping hot.

## TO FREEZE

Cool the completed
casserole (omitting
the parsley). Freeze for
up to 2 months. Thaw
thoroughly and reheat
until piping hot.

## TO COOK IN THE AGA

Brown the meat on the
Boiling Plate. At step
2 cover and transfer
to the Simmering Oven
for about 2 hours until
tender. Follow step 3
and again cover and
cook in the Simmering
Oven for a further
1–1½ hours or until
the meat is tender.

about 3 tablespoons
 sunflower oil
700g (1½ lb) stewing venison,
 cut into 2.5cm (1 in) pieces
700g (1½ lb) stewing beef,
 cut into 2.5cm (1 in) pieces
600g (1 lb 5 oz) shallots,
 left whole
2 garlic cloves, crushed
75g (3 oz) plain flour

1.1 litres (2 pints) beef stock
300ml (½ pint) red wine
2 tablespoons redcurrant jelly
salt and freshly ground
 black pepper
175g (6 oz) ready-to-eat
 dried apricots
150ml (¼ pint) port
chopped fresh parsley
 to garnish

Preheat the oven to 160°C/Fan 140°C/Gas 3.

**1** Heat the oil in a large, deep frying pan. Brown the
venison and beef in batches, adding more oil if necessary.
Lift the meat out of the pan, using a slotted spoon. Add
the whole shallots and garlic to the pan and cook, stirring
occasionally, until evenly browned. Lift out of the pan
with a slotted spoon.

**2** Lower the heat, then stir the flour into the oil left in
the pan, adding more if necessary, and cook for 1 minute.
Stir in the stock and red wine and bring to the boil,
stirring. Add the redcurrant jelly, and return the meat
and shallots to the pan. Season with salt and pepper,
bring to the boil, cover, then cook in the preheated
oven for 1½ hours.

**3** Add the apricots and port to the casserole. Return,
covered, to the oven and cook for 1 further hour until
the meat is tender. Adjust the seasoning and stir in
lots of parsley to serve.

COOK NOW, EAT LATER

✦

# Vegetarian
# Specials

CHAPTER FIVE

Flavour is perhaps the most vital element in vegetarian dishes. Although vegetables, pulses and grains are full of their own individual flavours, these are not strong, and need to be helped along by herbs, spices and often the vegetarian stand-by of cheese. Texture and colour are important too, so add crispness if you can in the form of a bit of celery or spring onion, and enliven the look of a dish with the bright colour of sweet peppers or fresh herbs.

I am very keen on meat-free meals and have really enjoyed cooking with beans, lentils and chickpeas, and have discovered how good most of the pulses available in cans are. All you need to do is open the can and rinse the contents! However, if I were cooking for a big event, I would always use dried pulses – soaking and cooking them – primarily because of the cost factor. But for small quantities, I heartily recommend tinned beans and chickpeas. So far as lentils are concerned, I like the French Puy, which are full of flavour themselves, but also absorb flavour from other ingredients while cooking. Couscous and bulgar wheat are also wonderful ingredients. They give texture to a dish and are perfect for use as a stuffing. When serving on the side, season and flavour well with herbs and finely chopped fresh vegetables.

You will notice that most of the recipes here are the vegetarian equivalent of conventional meat dishes. Most are now considered 'comfort' foods, and I wouldn't want vegetarians to miss out on those! I have not used meat substitutes, but the combinations of vegetables we have used make for a wonderful moussaka, cottage pie, lasagne and even sausages. Many vegetarian recipes can be cooked in advance, but the majority here – from a taste and texture point of view – are prepared well ahead and then cooked at the last minute. But with all that chopping, cutting, seeding, trimming and peeling out of the way, you will find cooking vegetarian very easy indeed!

SERVES 6

V

# Mediterranean Vegetable Galette with Mozzarella

A delicious puff pastry case filled with stir-fried vegetables. Ready-rolled puff pastry is easy to buy and even easier to use! The pastry border around the edge will rise up and frame the vegetables like a picture. It is essential to preheat the baking sheet as the bottom heat is needed to brown the pastry underneath the vegetables.

1 tablespoon olive oil
1 small aubergine, cut
   in half lengthways
   and thinly sliced
1 red onion, finely sliced
1 red pepper and 1 yellow
   pepper, seeded and cut
   into 2.5cm (1 in) cubes
1 small garlic clove, crushed
salt and freshly ground
   black pepper

1 × 375g (13 oz) packet
   ready-rolled puff pastry
100g (4 oz) Philadelphia
   full-fat cream cheese
1 tablespoon pesto,
   plus extra for drizzling
50g (2 oz) cherry
   tomatoes, halved
75g (3 oz) mozzarella
   cheese, coarsely grated
1 egg, beaten
fresh basil

Preheat the oven to 220°C/Fan 200°C/Gas 7. Put a large heavy baking sheet on a high shelf in the oven to preheat.

**1** Heat the oil in a deep frying pan, and stir-fry the aubergine until golden brown. Add the onion, peppers and garlic, and continue to stir-fry for about 5–10 minutes until the peppers are just cooked. Make sure that all the moisture has been driven off, over a high heat if necessary, otherwise the pastry will be soggy. Season with salt and pepper. Set aside to cool.

**2** Take the ready-rolled puff pastry and roll out a little bigger to a fairly thin rectangle about 25.5 × 38cm (10 × 15 in). Transfer to a sheet of foil and score a 4cm (1½ in) border around the edge of the pastry rectangle (score with a knife halfway through the pastry, do not cut right through). Using a sharp knife, diagonally mark around the border about every inch to give a pretty edge (again, do not cut right through). Prick the base of the pastry inside the border all over with a fork.

*Recipe continued overleaf*

**TO PREPARE AHEAD**
Cook the vegetables ahead. Cool, cover and keep in the fridge for up to 1 day. Roll and mark the pastry. Cover and keep in the fridge for 1 day. Mix the cheese and pesto, cover and keep in the fridge for up to 1 day. Assemble just before baking.

**TO FREEZE**
Not suitable.

## TO COOK IN THE AGA

The galette can be cooked on non-stick paper or a greased baking sheet (no need to preheat). Slide on to the floor of the Roasting Oven for about 10–15 minutes, or until the pastry rises around the vegetables and the base starts to brown. Transfer to the second set of runners of the Roasting Oven for about 8–10 minutes until the pastry is golden brown.

*Recipe continued*

**3** Mix the cream cheese in a bowl with the pesto and season with salt and pepper. Spread the cream cheese mixture evenly over the raw pastry, inside the marked border. Pile the cooled, cooked vegetables over the top of the cream cheese (again ensuring all is inside the border). Arrange the tomatoes (cut side up) on top of the vegetables and scatter over the mozzarella. Brush the pastry border with a little beaten egg. Take the baking sheet out of the oven and quickly slide the foil with the galette on top of the hot baking sheet. Return to the oven and bake for 20–25 minutes, or until the pastry rises around the vegetables and is a good golden brown.

**4** Scatter with basil, drizzle with pesto and serve with a fresh green salad.

# Bean Bangers

It is best to shape these sausages so that they are fairly short and fat rather than long and thin. They are then easier to cook, and won't break up.

**COOK NOW EAT LATER**

## TO PREPARE AHEAD
Prepare the sausages up to the end of step 2. Cover and keep in the fridge for up to 24 hours. Continue with step 3. You can also brown the sausages and reheat in a hot oven.

## TO FREEZE
Not suitable.

## TO COOK IN THE AGA
Brown the sausages in a frying pan on the Boiling Plate until golden, then transfer to a baking sheet and place on the second set of runners in the Roasting Oven for about 7–10 minutes until firm.

½ red onion, finely chopped
2 tablespoons chopped fresh parsley
1 teaspoon chopped fresh thyme
1 × 410g can cannellini beans, drained and rinsed
1 × 300g can red kidney beans, drained and rinsed
50g (2 oz) sun-dried tomatoes, coarsely chopped
50g (2 oz) Cheddar or mozzarella cheese, grated
2 tablespoons beaten egg
salt and freshly ground black pepper
50g (2 oz) fresh breadcrumbs
2–3 tablespoons olive oil

**1** Put the onion, parsley and thyme into a food processor and purée until fairly smooth. Add all the remaining ingredients, except the breadcrumbs and oil, to the processor and process until smooth.

**2** Shape the mixture into 12 sausages. Put the breadcrumbs on a large plate and then roll the sausages in them to coat evenly. Chill in the fridge for 30 minutes.

**3** Heat the oil in a large frying pan and brown the sausages until golden, turning carefully so that they do not break up. Lower the heat and continue to cook until the sausages are hot right through.

# Spinach and Feta Frittata

A frittata is a baked omelette, finished under the grill. Like an omelette, a frittata should not be overcooked. It is ideal for a light supper or for lunch. Serve with crusty bread and a salad.

6 eggs
4 tablespoons milk
salt and freshly ground
 black pepper
a little freshly grated nutmeg
a knob of butter
1 tablespoon sunflower oil
8 spring onions, sliced on
 the diagonal

100g (4 oz) closed-cup
 mushrooms
100g (4 oz) fresh baby
 spinach, coarsely sliced
75g (3 oz) feta cheese, diced
25g (1 oz) black olives in oil,
 drained and halved
a handful of fresh basil
 leaves, torn

**1** Blend together the eggs and milk in a bowl. Season with salt, pepper and nutmeg.

**2** Melt the butter and oil in a large non-stick frying pan and fry the spring onions and mushrooms over a high heat for a couple of minutes. Add the spinach, stir for 1 minute, then season.

**3** Pour the egg mixture into the pan and spread the spinach and mushroom mixture out through the egg. Sprinkle over the feta cheese and olives.

**4** Cook over a medium heat, loosening the edge with a spatula, for about 5–6 minutes until the base and edges of the mixture are set. Place under a preheated grill for a further 3–4 minutes or until the top is just set and golden brown.

**5** Invert the frittata on to a heated serving plate, cut into wedges and garnish with basil.

**COOK NOW
EAT LATER**

### TO PREPARE AHEAD
Prepare all the vegetables the day before, arrange on a plate in groups, cover with clingfilm and put in the fridge. Then the frittata will only take minutes to make. Or cook the frittata completely, turn out and allow to cool. Serve cold, cut into wedges for a summer lunch or picnic. Best made the same day, and not chilled.

### TO FREEZE
Not suitable.

### TO COOK IN THE AGA
Cook step 2 on the Boiling Plate. At step 3, transfer to the grid shelf on the second set of runners in the Roasting Oven for about 4–6 minutes until just set.

# Stir-fried Vegetable Lasagne

**V** **SERVES 6**

There is no lengthy sauce-making process for this lasagne. The 'sauce' is simply mascarpone and ricotta cheeses mixed together with single cream and plenty of seasoning. It is fairly rich so only needs to be spread thinly for each layer.

**COOK NOW EAT LATER**

**TO PREPARE AHEAD**
Complete to the end of step 4. Cool, cover and keep in the fridge for up to 2 days. Cook as in step 5, but for a little longer, about 50 minutes.

**TO FREEZE**
Freeze the dish prepared up to the end of step 4, well wrapped, for up to a month. To thaw, defrost in the fridge overnight, and cook as in step 5, but for a little longer, about 50 minutes.

3 tablespoons olive oil
2 large onions, roughly chopped
3 garlic cloves, crushed
350g (12 oz) chestnut mushrooms, sliced
1 aubergine, cut into sugar-cube-sized pieces
1 red pepper, seeded and roughly chopped
1 tablespoon plain flour
1 × 400g can chopped tomatoes
2 tablespoons chopped fresh parsley
salt and freshly ground black pepper

100g (4 oz) Emmental cheese, grated
150g (5 oz) dried pre-cooked lasagne sheets
50g (2 oz) Parmesan or Parmesan-style hard cheese, freshly grated

**Quick Sauce**
1 × 250g tub full-fat mascarpone cheese
1 × 250g tub full-fat ricotta cheese
300ml (½ pint) single cream

Preheat the oven to 190°C/Fan 170°C/Gas 5. You will need a shallow ovenproof dish about 25.5 × 23cm (10 × 9 in).

**1** Heat the oil in a large frying pan, add the onions and garlic, and cook over a high heat, stirring from time to time, for about 4–5 minutes. Add the mushrooms, aubergine and red pepper and cook, stirring over a high heat, for 2–3 minutes. Lower the heat, cover the pan and cook for about 20 minutes, until the aubergine is tender.

**2** Blend the flour with the juices from the can of tomatoes in a bowl, and mix until smooth. Add with the tomatoes, parsley and seasoning to the vegetable mixture, and stir well. Cover again and simmer for a further 10–15 minutes. Check the seasoning.

**3** For the sauce, simply mix together the mascarpone and ricotta cheeses with the cream and season well with salt and pepper.

**4** To assemble, spread one-third of the mushroom and aubergine mixture over the base, then one-third of the sauce and a third of the Emmental. Cover with a single layer of half the lasagne sheets and then repeat these layers once more. Top with a final layer of the mushroom and aubergine mixture, the sauce and Emmental, and finish with the Parmesan.

**5** Cook in the preheated oven for about 40 minutes until the top is golden and bubbling, and the lasagne is piping hot.

**6** Serve with crusty bread and a fresh green salad.

**TO COOK IN THE AGA**
Cook the onions and garlic on the Boiling Plate. Add the mushrooms, aubergine and red pepper, cover and transfer to the Simmering Oven for 25 minutes. Blend in the flour, tomatoes, parsley and seasoning, bring to the boil, cover and return to the Simmering Oven for about 10–15 minutes. Complete steps 3 and 4 then cook on the second set of runners in the Roasting Oven for about 35–45 minutes until cooked through and golden brown.

# Spiced Lentil and Tomato Moussaka

*You need not be a vegetarian to enjoy this dish. It is rich in flavour and, with the added red peppers and tomatoes, colourful too. Buy dried French Puy lentils in packets, and add as they are.*

**COOK NOW EAT LATER**

## TO PREPARE AHEAD

Assemble the moussaka as in step 5, but don't cook in the oven yet. Cool, cover and keep in the fridge for up to 1 day. Cook from room temperature in the oven at the same temperature as above for 40–50 minutes until golden on top and piping hot right through.

## TO FREEZE

Cover and freeze the assembled, but not oven-cooked, moussaka for up to 3 months. Thaw overnight in the fridge and cook as above.

6 tablespoons olive oil
2 large onions, roughly chopped
3 large garlic cloves, crushed
2 large red peppers, seeded and chopped into large pieces
225g (8 oz) dried Puy lentils
3 × 400g cans chopped tomatoes
300ml (½ pint) vegetable stock
1–2 tablespoons mango chutney

salt and freshly ground black pepper
3 large aubergines, thickly sliced, about 5mm (¼ in)

**Cheese Sauce**
50g (2 oz) butter
50g (2 oz) plain flour
600ml (1 pint) milk
225g (8 oz) mature Cheddar, grated
2 teaspoons Dijon mustard
freshly grated nutmeg to taste

Preheat the oven to 200°C/Fan 180°C/Gas 6, and lightly grease a large, shallow, ovenproof dish, about 25 × 33cm (10 × 13 in).

**1** Heat 2 tablespoons of the olive oil in a large sauté pan. Add the onions, garlic and peppers and cook gently for about 4–5 minutes until beginning to soften.

**2** Add the lentils, tomatoes, vegetable stock, mango chutney and seasoning. Cover and simmer for about 40–60 minutes or until the lentils are cooked. Check the seasoning.

**3** Brush the sliced aubergines with the remaining olive oil and season with salt and pepper. Arrange in a single layer on a baking sheet and place under a hot grill for about 2–3 minutes each side, until the slices are golden brown (you will have to do this in batches).

**4** Next make the cheese sauce. Melt the butter in a medium saucepan, take off the heat and stir in the flour. Return to a low heat, stirring, for 2–3 minutes, then again remove from the heat and gradually add the milk. Bring up to the boil, stirring, and simmer for about 2 minutes. Add 175g (6 oz) of the cheese, the mustard, nutmeg and some salt and pepper.

**5** To assemble the moussaka, spoon half of the lentil mixture into the dish, cover with half of the cheese sauce and arrange half of the aubergine slices on top. Repeat with the remaining lentil mixture, cheese sauce and aubergine, and finally sprinkle with the remaining Cheddar.

**6** Cook in the preheated oven for about 30–40 minutes or until golden on top and piping hot.

**7** Serve with crusty bread and a fresh green salad.

**TO COOK IN THE AGA**
Cook the lentils to the end of step 2 in the Simmering Oven for about 1¼ hours. Cook the aubergines on the highest set of runners in the Roasting Oven for 3–5 minutes on each side. Make the sauce on the Simmering Plate. Cook the assembled dish on the grid shelf on the floor of the Roasting Oven for about 30–40 minutes.

# Chunky Vegetable Thai Curry

A delicious vegetable curry suitable for vegetarians and meat-eaters alike!

**SERVES 6**

**V**

**COOK NOW EAT LATER**

## TO PREPARE AHEAD
Steps 1 and 2 can be done up to 12 hours ahead.

## TO FREEZE
Not suitable.

## TO COOK IN THE AGA
Soften the onion for 10 minutes, covered in the Simmering Oven. Continue with steps 1 and 2, bring to boil on the Boiling Plate, and transfer to the Simmering Oven for 10 minutes until the vegetables are tender. Follow steps 3 and 4, cover and transfer to the Simmering Oven for a further 10–15 minutes until tender.

2 tablespoons sunflower oil
1 large onion, chopped into large pieces
2 fat garlic cloves, crushed
1 fat small green chilli, seeded and chopped
about 2.5cm (1 in) piece root ginger, grated
finely grated zest of ½ lime
1 tablespoon ground coriander
1 tablespoon ground cumin
1 tablespoon garam masala
175g (6 oz) sweet potatoes, peeled and cut into batons
175g (6 oz) parsnips, peeled and cut into batons

450ml (¾ pint) vegetable stock
1 × 400ml can coconut milk
salt and freshly ground black pepper
175g (6 oz) runner beans, cut into 1cm (½ in) pieces
100g (4 oz) large-cup mushrooms, quartered
½ red pepper, seeded and thinly sliced
100g (4 oz) baby sweetcorn, cut lengthways
1 × 400g can flageolet beans, drained and rinsed
juice of 1 lime
fresh coriander leaves

**1** Heat the oil in a large, deep frying pan and fry the onion for about 10 minutes over a low heat until starting to soften. Add the garlic, chilli, ginger and lime zest to the onion and stir-fry for 2–3 minutes. Add the spices, mix well and cook for 1 minute over a high heat.

**2** Stir in the sweet potatoes and parsnips, blend in the stock and coconut milk and season with salt and pepper. Bring to the boil, stirring, cover and simmer over a low heat for about 10–15 minutes until the vegetables are nearly tender.

**3** Blanch the runner beans in a pan of boiling salted water for about 4 minutes until al dente. Drain and refresh in cold water until completely cold. Set aside to dry.

**4** Add the mushrooms, red pepper, sweetcorn, flageolet beans and dry, blanched runner beans to the pan, stir well and bring back to the boil for 1 minute. Cover and continue to cook over a low heat for a further 10–15 minutes until all the vegetables are tender. Check the seasoning, add the lime juice and coriander and serve with rice.

# Herb Falafels

A quick and easy supper dish, and the falafels can be made any shape
or size you like. For a starter, little tiny ones look very effective.

2 × 410g cans chickpeas,
  drained
2 teaspoons ground cumin
1 teaspoon ground turmeric
1 teaspoon cayenne pepper
1 garlic clove, crushed
1 × 28g packet fresh
  coriander, leaves and stalks

2–3 tablespoons olive oil
salt and freshly ground
  black pepper

**To Finish**
a little plain flour for coating
a little vegetable oil for frying

**1** Measure all the falafel ingredients, except for the olive
oil and seasoning, into a food processor. Process until
blended, but still with a coarse texture. Add the olive oil
and process again to mix. Season with salt and pepper.

**2** Shape into 12 ovals about 7.5cm (3 in) long and 1cm
(½ in) deep. Transfer to the fridge for at least 1 hour,
if time allows, to firm up.

**3** Coat with a little flour ready for frying.

**4** Heat a frying pan until very hot, add a little oil and fry
the falafels for about 5 minutes on each side, until golden
brown and hot right through. Transfer to kitchen paper
for a moment before serving.

**5** Serve with warmed flat bread, a herby green salad,
chopped tomatoes and yoghurt.

## TO PREPARE AHEAD

After step 2, the falafels
can be put into the
fridge up to 24 hours
ahead. Then follow
step 3 onwards to cook
and serve. Otherwise,
cool after step 4 and
put in the fridge up to
24 hours ahead. Either
quickly fry them to
reheat, or put in a hot
oven at 200°C/Fan
180°C/Gas 6 for about
10–15 minutes.

## TO FREEZE

Not suitable.

## TO COOK IN THE AGA

Cook in a hot frying
pan on the Boiling
Plate. If cooked in
advance, reheat on
a baking sheet on
the floor of the
Roasting Oven for
about 10 minutes
until piping hot.

# Lentil and Vegetable Cottage Pie

This idea was very popular when we were trying it out. It tastes delicious and the ingredients are inexpensive, which makes it a cheap meal to cook.

**COOK NOW EAT LATER**

## TO PREPARE AHEAD

Make ahead to the end of step 6. Cool, cover and keep in the fridge for up to 24 hours. Complete step 7 to serve, cooking for about 40 minutes.

## TO FREEZE

Not suitable.

2 large onions, finely chopped
2 garlic cloves, crushed
2 tablespoons olive oil
3 celery sticks, sliced
2 large carrots, sliced
100g (4 oz) dried red lentils, rinsed
1 × 400g can chopped tomatoes
300ml (½ pint) vegetable stock
2 teaspoons sun-dried tomato paste

50g (2 oz) sun-dried tomatoes, drained if in oil, and chopped
salt and freshly ground black pepper

**Topping**
1kg (2¼ lb) potatoes, peeled
about 150ml (¼ pint) milk
a bunch of spring onions, finely chopped
25g (1 oz) butter
175g (6 oz) mature Cheddar cheese, grated

Preheat the oven to 200°C/Fan 180°C/Gas 6. You will need an ovenproof dish, about 28 × 23 × 5cm (11 × 9 × 2 in).

**1** Cook the onions and garlic in the oil over a low heat in a large pan for about 10 minutes until soft. Add the celery and carrots and cook for a further 5 minutes.

**2** Stir in the lentils, then add the chopped tomatoes, stock, tomato paste, sun-dried tomatoes and plenty of seasoning. Bring to the boil, cover and simmer for about 20 minutes until the vegetables are tender. Check the seasoning.

**3** Meanwhile, cook the potatoes in boiling salted water until tender.

**4** While the potatoes are cooking, heat the milk and spring onions together in a small pan and simmer gently for about 5 minutes until the spring onions are soft.

**5** Drain the potatoes well, then add the warm milk with the spring onions and the butter. Mash together adding plenty of salt and pepper. Stir in two-thirds of the grated cheese and check the seasoning.

**6** Spoon the vegetable mixture into the prepared dish and gently spread the potato on top. Scatter the remaining cheese over the top of the potato.

**7** Cook in the preheated oven for about 30 minutes until the potato is golden and the sauce bubbling.

### TO COOK IN THE AGA

Cook the onions, etc. firstly on the Boiling Plate, then transfer, covered, to the Simmering Oven for 30 minutes or until tender. Cook the potatoes on the Boiling Plate. Cook the assembled dish on a high shelf in the Roasting Oven for about 20 minutes until golden brown and piping hot.

# Roasted Field Mushrooms
## with Couscous and Feta

If you are keen on goat's cheese, use that instead of the feta. Choose a firm goat's cheese that can be cut into cubes. Serve with a mixed salad.

12 large flat mushrooms
2–3 tablespoons olive oil
a knob of butter
salt and freshly ground
  black pepper
3 very large tomatoes, each
  cut into 4 thick slices
1 medium onion, finely
  chopped

1 garlic clove, crushed
225g (8 oz) couscous
300ml (½ pint) vegetable
  stock
400g (14 oz) feta cheese,
  cubed
about 3 tablespoons chopped
  fresh parsley, plus more
  to garnish

**COOK NOW
EAT LATER**

**TO PREPARE AHEAD**
Prepare to the end of
step 4. Cover and keep
in the fridge for up to
24 hours. Cook as in
step 5.

**TO FREEZE**
Not suitable.

**TO COOK IN THE AGA**
Fry the mushrooms
in a pan on the Boiling
Plate for a couple of
minutes on each side.
Remove to an ovenproof
dish. Add the slices of
tomato to the pan and
cook for 1 minute. Put
on to the mushrooms.
Follow step 4. Bake
on the second set of
runners in the Roasting
Oven for about 15–20
minutes until hot
through and tinged
with brown.

Preheat the oven to 200°C/Fan 180°C/Gas 6.

**1** Remove the central stalks from the mushrooms. Heat half the oil in a large frying pan, add the butter and cook the mushrooms lightly, turning until nearly tender. (You may need to do this in batches.) Remove the mushrooms to a large shallow ovenproof dish (or two smaller dishes), large enough to hold the mushrooms in a single layer. Season with salt and pepper.

**2** Lightly fry the 12 thick slices of tomato, season and put on top of the mushrooms.

**3** Heat the remaining oil in the pan. Add the onion and garlic and cook until soft, about 10 minutes.

**4** Meanwhile, measure the couscous into a bowl, pour over the boiling stock and leave to soak until all the stock has been absorbed. Add the cooked onion and garlic to the couscous, lightly stir in the cheese cubes and parsley, and season (go easy on the salt as feta is salty). Divide between the mushrooms in the dish.

**5** Cook in the preheated oven for about 20–30 minutes until hot through and the cheese cubes are bubbling and tinged with brown. Scatter with more parsley to serve.

# Stuffed Peppers
## with Halloumi and Olives

V SERVES 6

Ideal for a light lunch. Serve with crusty bread to soak up the juices
and perhaps a green salad. Mozzarella can be used instead of halloumi.

## TO PREPARE AHEAD
Cook and cool the
mushroom and bean
mixture, then use
to fill the peppers.
Complete step 3, cover
and keep in the fridge
for up to 8 hours.

## TO FREEZE
Not suitable.

## TO COOK IN THE AGA
Cook the onion and
mushrooms on the
Boiling Plate. Loosely
cover the assembled
dish with foil and slide
on to the grid shelf
on the floor of the
Roasting Oven for
about 30 minutes.
Remove the foil and
cook for a further 20
minutes or until the
peppers are tender
and the cheese is
golden and bubbling.

6 large red peppers
salt and freshly ground
   black pepper
2 tablespoons olive oil
1 medium onion, finely
   chopped
1 garlic clove, crushed
225g (8 oz) chestnut
   mushrooms, sliced

2 × 300g cans flageolet
   beans, rinsed and drained
about 24 black olives, stoned
about 2 tablespoons roughly
   chopped fresh basil
1 × 250g pack halloumi
   cheese, coarsely grated
fresh basil leaves
   to garnish

Preheat the oven to 180°C/Fan 160°C/Gas 4. Lightly
oil a large, shallow ovenproof dish, large enough to fit
12 pepper halves snugly in a single layer (or two smaller
shallow dishes).

**1** Cut the peppers in half lengthways, leaving the green
stalk but removing the seeds. Put into the ovenproof
dish and season lightly.

**2** Heat the oil in a medium pan, add the onion and garlic
and cook gently for 5–10 minutes until soft. Add the
mushrooms and continue to cook until tender. Add the
beans and olives to the pan and season to taste.

**3** Divide the bean and mushroom mixture between the
pepper halves, scatter with the chopped basil and top
with the cheese.

**4** Bake in the preheated oven for about 1 hour until the
peppers are tender and the cheese golden and bubbling.
Scatter with basil leaves to serve.

# Pasta Primavera

A fresh, fairly healthy – and meat-free – pasta recipe,
using bright, colourful vegetables.

**COOK NOW
EAT LATER**

## TO PREPARE AHEAD

The roast vegetables
can be roasted well
ahead of time, or
even the day before,
and reheated in a hot
oven as you boil the
pasta. If liked, the
pasta can be cooked,
drained, refreshed
and covered up to
6 hours in advance.
As can the broccoli
and asparagus: boil
in salted water for
3 minutes then
plunge into cold
water and drain.

## TO FREEZE

Not suitable.

## TO COOK IN THE AGA

Roast the onions and
red peppers on the
floor of the Roasting
Oven for 30 minutes,
turning from time
to time. Add the
courgettes after
15 minutes. Cook
everything else on
the Boiling Plate.

2 tablespoons olive oil
2 large onions, halved
    and thickly sliced
2 red peppers, seeded
    and cut into large pieces
salt and freshly ground
    black pepper
350g (12 oz) small
    courgettes, thickly sliced
350g (12 oz) dried tagliatelle

225g (8 oz) broccoli florets
225g (8 oz) asparagus tips
200ml (7 fl oz) full-fat
    crème fraîche
3–4 tablespoons pesto,
    according to taste
50g (2 oz) Parmesan or
    Parmesan-style hard
    cheese, freshly grated

Preheat the oven to 220°C/Fan 200°C/Gas 7.

**1** Measure the oil into a large polythene bag, add the
onions and red peppers and season well. Toss together,
then turn into a large roasting tin and roast in the
preheated oven, turning from time to time, for about
40 minutes, until the vegetables are just done. Add
the courgettes after 20 minutes as they take less
time to cook.

**2** Boil the pasta in salted water according to the packet
instructions, usually about 10 minutes, adding the
broccoli and asparagus for the last 3 minutes. Drain
and leave in the colander while making the sauce.

**3** Heat the crème fraîche and pesto together in the pasta
saucepan. Return the pasta and roasted vegetables to
the pan, and toss together, adding some of the Parmesan.

**4** Serve immediately in a heated dish, sprinkled with
the remaining Parmesan.

# Pistou Pasta with Rocket

A very simple recipe, which will take just 15 minutes to make from scratch – but you can prepare ahead as well. Serve with a green leaf salad.

350g (12 oz) dried penne pasta
150ml (¼ pint) white wine
2 shallots, finely chopped
450g (1 lb) mixed wild
mushrooms, coarsely sliced
salt and freshly ground
black pepper
4 tablespoons pouring
double cream
1 × 50g (2 oz) bag rocket,
removing some of the end
stalks to add to the pistou
coarsely grated Parmesan or
Parmesan-style hard
cheese, to serve

**Pistou**

a very good handful of fresh
basil (leaves and stalks)
1 fat garlic clove, peeled
rocket stalks (see above)
about 4 tablespoons olive oil

**COOK NOW EAT LATER**

### TO PREPARE AHEAD

Chop the shallots and slice the mushrooms up to 8 hours ahead. Make the pistou, cover and keep in the fridge for up to 24 hours. You could cook, drain, refresh, cover and chill the pasta up to 6 hours ahead.

### TO FREEZE

Not suitable.

### TO COOK IN THE AGA

Use the Boiling Plate to cook the mushrooms and the pasta.

**1** First boil a pan of salted water for the pasta. When boiling, add the pasta and cook for about 12 minutes, or according to packet instructions.

**2** Meanwhile, make the pistou by measuring the basil, garlic and rocket stalks into a food processor and processing quickly. Add the olive oil and process again. The oil doesn't mix well but it takes on the flavour of the garlic and herbs.

**3** Boil the wine in a large frying pan with the shallots and reduce for a few minutes. Add all of the mushrooms and stir over a high heat for a few minutes until the mushrooms are cooked and the liquid has reduced to roughly 2 tablespoons. Season with salt and pepper. Add the cream and pistou, stirring to mix.

**4** Drain the pasta and add to the mushroom mixture in the pan. Check the seasoning.

**5** At the last moment stir in the rocket leaves, and then serve with the Parmesan.

COOK NOW, EAT LATER

✸

# Vegetables and Salads

CHAPTER SIX

One usually thinks of a salad as being a last-minute job, but with many salad vegetables you can prepare them – and even dress them – some hours in advance. Even if you are using fragile salad vegetables, you can prepare ahead to a certain extent. With something as simple as a green salad, put the dressing in the bottom of the salad bowl, then add the 'tougher', crisper vegetables – shreds of fennel or celery, say, which might benefit from marinating. Turn in the dressing, then pile the lettuce leaves on top, but don't stir. Clingfilm the top and put in the fridge for up to 8 hours. The salad will be chilled and crisp when you come to mix it all together, and not soggy from tossing too early. I think you'll agree that takes quite a lot of the pressure off you, if you are busy with other stages of a meal.

Vegetables, too, one thinks of as a last-minute thing, and many green vegetables are undeniably best when freshly boiled briefly in salted water. (I do not recommend steaming green vegetables as they lose their bright green colour.) But several dishes can be prepared well in advance and cooked at the last moment. You could part-cook roasted vegetables until golden the day before. I do this with roots mainly – with a mixture as on page 162, or with potatoes and parsnips to go with a roast joint. Then all you have to do on the day is blast them in a very hot oven to get them brown and crisp just before serving.

# Pot-roasted Roots
## with Rosemary

V SERVES 6

A prepare-ahead vegetable dish that needs very little last-minute attention. Vary it with other English root vegetables, such as turnips and swede. If you can't get shallots, use small onions, cutting them in half if need be.

**TO PREPARE AHEAD**
Par-roast the vegetables the day before at step 3 for about 30 minutes until under-brown. Complete the roasting in a preheated oven at the same temperature for about 30 minutes until piping hot, golden brown and crisp.

**TO FREEZE**
Not suitable.

**TO COOK IN THE AGA**
Cook the vegetables in the prepared roasting tin on the floor of the Roasting Oven for about 40 minutes, turning from time to time, until tender, piping hot, golden brown and crisp.

350g (12 oz) parsnips, peeled (prepared weight)
350g (12 oz) celeriac, peeled (prepared weight)
350g (12 oz) tiny shallots, peeled and left whole (prepared weight)
350g (12 oz) carrots, peeled (prepared weight)

olive oil
salt and freshly ground black pepper
a large sprig of fresh rosemary
chopped fresh parsley

Line a large roasting tin with foil and brush with oil. Preheat the oven to 200°C/Fan 180°C/Gas 6.

**1** Cut the parsnips and celeriac into neat pieces a similar size to the shallots. Slice the carrots on the diagonal (these should be smaller as they take longer to cook).

**2** Bring the vegetables to the boil in salted water, and simmer for 5 minutes. Drain, coat with 2–3 tablespoons of oil and season well.

**3** Tip the vegetables into the prepared roasting tin and add the rosemary. Roast in the preheated oven for about 40–50 minutes, turning from time to time, until tender, piping hot, golden brown and crisp.

**4** Serve sprinkled with parsley.

# Chilled Mediterranean Salad

**V** SERVES 6

A colourful salad to enjoy in summer. It's essential that you serve it chilled. It's also good on individual plates as a summer first course, nice with warm bread or rolls.

550g (1 ¼ lb) ripe tomatoes
   (about 6 large)
salt and freshly ground
   black pepper
1 medium cucumber
1 small mild onion
1 medium red pepper
2 small Little Gem lettuces,
   broken in small pieces
2 tablespoons roughly
   chopped fresh flat-leaf
   parsley
leaves from a few sprigs
   of fresh basil
about 18 black olives (optional)
a few shavings of Parmesan

**Croûtons**
2 slices thick white bread,
   crust removed
2 tablespoons good olive oil
2 fat garlic cloves, crushed

**Dressing**
3 tablespoons good olive oil
1 tablespoon lemon juice
1 teaspoon caster sugar
1 tablespoon balsamic vinegar
a few shavings of Parmesan
   or Parmesan-style
   hard cheese

COOK NOW
EAT LATER

**TO PREPARE AHEAD**
Make the salad to the end of step 4 up to 8 hours ahead, and keep in the fridge. The croûtons and dressing can be made a day ahead, no need to chill. Just before the meal shake the dressing, pour over the salad, arrange on the serving plate and garnish.

**TO FREEZE**
Not suitable.

**1** Slice off the ends of the tomatoes thinly and cut each tomato into 3 slices, then slice each round into about 6 wedges. Transfer to a fairly large bowl, season with pepper but don't stir as the tomatoes will break up.

**2** Cut the cucumber in half lengthways. Remove the seeds with a melon bailer or teaspoon, or simply push your thumb nail firmly down the centre of the cucumber from one end to the other. Discard the seeds. Cut the cucumber in slices about the thickness of medium-sliced bread. Add the horseshoe cucumber shapes to the bowl.

**3** Peel and cut the onion in 4, then cut each wedge into very fine slices (not cutting through the root) which will fall apart into bow shapes. Add to the bowl.

*Recipe continued overleaf*

**COOK NOW EAT LATER**

**TO COOK IN THE AGA**
Bake the croûtons on the top set of runners in the Roasting Oven in a foil-lined roasting tin. Watch carefully and turn frequently.

*Recipe continued*

**4** Seed the pepper and cut into fine julienne strips. Add with the lettuce to the bowl but do not mix together. Cover with clingfilm and chill for 6 hours ideally.

**5** Meanwhile, make the croûtons and dressing. Cut the bread into rough cubes, and put in a polythene bag with the oil, garlic and a little pepper. Gently shake to evenly coat with the oil. Either put in a foil-lined grill pan and toast under the grill until golden, or brown in a hot oven (about 220°C/Fan 200°C/Gas 7), watching carefully.

**6** For the dressing, just blend the ingredients in a small bowl, and season with salt and pepper.

**7** Take the large bowl from the fridge. Arrange the lettuce as a base for the salad on a serving plate, and add a little salt. Gently toss the rest of the salad in the bowl with the dressing and croûtons and a little salt. Pile on the serving plate and add the parsley, basil, olives and Parmesan.

# Green Leaf Salad
## with Pomegranate and Pumpkin Seeds and a Mint Dressing

A fresh leafy salad with the added crunch of pumpkin seeds and pomegranate. To make it a main salad for a summer's lunch, add 175g (6 oz) crumbled feta cheese.

**COOK NOW EAT LATER**

### TO PREPARE AHEAD
The salad can be arranged in the dish up to 6 hours ahead. Pour the dressing over to serve.

### TO FREEZE
Not suitable.

1 head romaine lettuce
1 head red chicory
2 large handfuls
    lamb's lettuce
1–2 teaspoons olive oil
50g (2 oz) pumpkin seeds
2 teaspoons sea salt
100g (4 oz) pomegranate seeds
    (½ a medium-sized fruit)

**Mint Dressing**
juice of ½ lemon
½ teaspoon Dijon mustard
3 tablespoons olive oil
1 tablespoon chopped
    fresh chives
1 tablespoon chopped
    fresh mint
1 heaped teaspoon sugar
salt and freshly ground
    black pepper

**1** Break the leaves from the romaine lettuce and chicory and wash to remove any dirt. Break the romaine leaves into large manageable-sized pieces and arrange in a dish with the chicory. Scatter over the lamb's lettuce.

**2** Heat the oil in a non-stick frying pan, add the pumpkin seeds and sea salt and fry for about 6–8 minutes until coated in salt and crisp.

**3** To make the dressing, mix the ingredients together in a bowl and whisk until smooth.

**4** Scatter the pomegranate and pumpkin seeds over the green leaves and pour over the dressing to serve.

# Quinoa and Rocket Salad
## with a Garlic Dressing

SERVES 6

Quinoa is a seed high in protein and low in gluten. Treat it in a similar way to bulgar wheat or couscous. It makes a healthy salad with an interesting texture.

200g (7 oz) quinoa
500ml (18 fl oz) water
1 × 400g can chickpeas,
    drained and rinsed
1 × 195g can sweetcorn,
    drained
4 celery stalks, thinly
    sliced on the diagonal
6 thin spring onions,
    trimmed and finely chopped
salt and freshly ground
    black pepper

**Rocket and Garlic
    Dressing**
2 garlic cloves, crushed
50g (2 oz) fresh rocket
small bunch flat-leaf parsley
small bunch fresh basil
12 tablespoons extra
    virgin olive oil
juice and zest of 1 large lemon

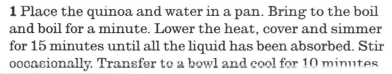

**COOK NOW
EAT LATER**

### TO PREPARE AHEAD
Make up to 12 hours ahead for all the flavours to infuse. If it is made too far ahead the bright green colour from the herbs will fade.

### TO FREEZE
Not suitable.

### TO COOK IN THE AGA
Bake on the grid shelf on the floor of the Roasting Oven, with the cold sheet on the second set of runners, for about 25 minutes.

**1** Place the quinoa and water in a pan. Bring to the boil and boil for a minute. Lower the heat, cover and simmer for 15 minutes until all the liquid has been absorbed. Stir occasionally. Transfer to a bowl and cool for 10 minutes.

**2** Stir in the chickpeas, sweetcorn, celery and spring onions and season well with salt and pepper. Leave to cool further.

**3** To make the dressing, place all the ingredients in a food processor and whiz until fairly smooth but with a little texture. Otherwise, chop the herbs and then whisk all the ingredients together thoroughly. Season well and stir into the salad. Check the seasoning and serve.

# Grainy Mustard and Herb Potato Salad

Potato salad is always a favourite for a buffet. This is a delicious variation with a slightly lighter dressing.

## TO PREPARE AHEAD
Prepare to the end of step 3 up to 48 hours ahead. The mayonnaise and herbs can be mixed up to 48 hours in advance but do not mix this with the potatoes until about 10 hours ahead.

## TO FREEZE
Not suitable.

## TO COOK IN THE AGA
Use the Boiling Plate to cook the potatoes and the onion.

1kg (2¼ lb) baby
  new potatoes
1 large mild onion,
  thinly sliced
salt and freshly ground
  black pepper
6 tablespoons 'light'
  low-calorie mayonnaise
2 tablespoons snipped
  fresh chives
1 tablespoon chopped
  fresh parsley

**Vinaigrette**
1½ tablespoons grainy
  mustard
2 tablespoons white
  wine vinegar
1 tablespoon lemon juice
1 teaspoon caster sugar
6 tablespoons olive oil

**1** Slice the new potatoes in half lengthways. Boil with the onion in salted water for about 15 minutes until just tender. Drain and set aside for about 5 minutes.

**2** While the potatoes are cooking, make the vinaigrette. Mix all the ingredients together in a bowl and blend together by hand with a whisk. Season with salt and pepper.

**3** When the potatoes have cooled for about 5 minutes (i.e. they should still be warm), pour over the vinaigrette, stir and set aside to cool.

**4** Mix the mayonnaise and herbs together in a small bowl and mix into the cold potatoes.

# Celeriac and Fresh Herb Salad

Celeriac is a wonderful vegetable, particularly delicious as a purée. It has a thick layer of peel on the outside so it needs to be peeled with a knife not a peeler. It is necessary to blanch the flesh because as soon as cut celeriac is exposed to the air it turns brown. If you prefer a creamy dressing, add 4 tablespoons mayonnaise to the dressing.

**TO PREPARE AHEAD**
Steps 1, 2 and 3 can be prepared up to 48 hours ahead but keep the vegetables separate. The completed dressed salad can be made up to 8 hours ahead.

**TO FREEZE**
Not suitable.

1 celeriac, weighing about 450g (1 lb)
salt and freshly ground black pepper
1 large carrot, peeled

**Dressing**
juice of 1 lemon
4 tablespoons olive oil
¼ teaspoon caster sugar

2 tablespoons chopped fresh basil
2 tablespoons snipped fresh chives
2 tablespoons chopped fresh parsley

**1** Peel and shred the celeriac into very fine strips, about 7.5cm (3 in) long. Blanch in boiling salted water for about 1½ minutes, then refresh in cold water and drain well.

**2** Cut the carrot into fine strips about 7.5cm (3 in) long. No need to blanch.

**3** Whisk the lemon juice, oil, sugar and some salt and pepper together in a small bowl, then stir in the herbs.

**4** Mix the shredded vegetables with the dressing, check the seasoning and spoon into a serving dish.

# Red Cabbage
## with Lemony Coleslaw Dressing

A variation on a classic coleslaw. There were great discussions here as to whether we liked the colour or not. Some of us loved it, some weren't too sure! It is quite pink, so if you are worried about this, use a white cabbage instead.

1 red cabbage, weighing
   about 450g (1 lb)
3 small celery sticks
2 carrots, peeled
½ mild onion, very finely
   sliced
50g (2 oz) walnut pieces
   (optional)
50g (2 oz) sultanas (optional)
salt and freshly ground
   black pepper
2 tablespoons chopped
   fresh parsley

**Sauce**
4 tablespoons 'light'
   low-calorie mayonnaise
4 tablespoons half-fat
   crème fraîche
juice of 1 lemon
2 teaspoons Dijon mustard
1 teaspoon caster sugar
2 tablespoons hot water

**TO PREPARE AHEAD**
All the vegetables
can be prepared up
to 2 days ahead. The
sauce can be made
up to 2 days ahead
as well, but keep the
two separate. Mix
together up to 4
hours before serving.

**TO FREEZE**
Not suitable.

**1** Cut the cabbage into quarters and remove the core. Shred the cabbage, celery and carrots into very fine strips (about 6cm/2½ in long) and add the sliced onion. This can be done in a food processor if preferred.

**2** Mix all the vegetables together in a large bowl and stir in the walnuts and sultanas, if using. Season with salt and pepper.

**3** Mix the sauce ingredients together in a small bowl until smooth. Pour over the vegetables and mix together, until all are coated. Check the seasoning.

**4** Stir in the parsley, and turn into a serving dish. Serve at room temperature.

# Hot Cajun-spiced Potato Wedges

A quick recipe to serve as a snack, or before supper.
Good dipped in soured cream or tomato salsa.

**COOK NOW
EAT LATER**

**TO PREPARE AHEAD**
Prepare the potato
wedges in the
marinade up to
8 hours ahead.

**TO FREEZE**
Not suitable.

**TO COOK IN THE AGA**
Slide the tin on the
grid shelf on the
floor of the Roasting
Oven for about 25–30
minutes, turning
occasionally so they
are golden brown
all over.

2 large potatoes, scrubbed
1 tablespoon sunflower oil
1 teaspoon runny honey
½ garlic clove, crushed
½ teaspoon ground coriander
½ teaspoon allspice powder
½ teaspoon chilli powder
salt and freshly ground
    black pepper

Preheat the oven to 200°C/Fan 180°C/Gas 6. Line a small
roasting tin with foil or non-stick paper.

**1** Cut the potatoes into decent-sized wedges, leaving the
skin on. Mix all the other ingredients together in a bowl,
toss in the potato wedges and toss until well coated. Tip
the wedges into the lined roasting tin.

**2** Bake in the preheated oven for about 30–40 minutes,
giving the tin a little shake halfway through so the
potatoes do not stick. They should be cooked through
and golden brown and crisp. (The timing depends on
the size of your wedges.) Sprinkle with salt and pepper.

**3** Serve immediately with a dip made simply from
a mixture of soured cream and snipped chives.

# Majorcan Tumbet

There is no translation for this classic Majorcan dish. It is a mix of roasted Mediterranean vegetables, potatoes and tomato. My first encounter with it was when we arrived in Majorca to stay with some dear friends. Miranda had made Tumbet with added chicken and we ate it outside as the sun went down. It's good with barbecues, roast meats, grills or pan-fries. It will keep hot for about 40 minutes.

500g (1 lb 2 oz) aubergines
600g (1 lb 6 oz) baby new
  potatoes, scrubbed
500g (1 lb 2 oz) Spanish
  onions, thickly sliced
3 fat garlic cloves, left whole
salt and freshly ground
  black pepper

2 large red peppers,
  halved and seeded
olive oil
2 teaspoons chopped
  fresh rosemary
400ml (14 fl oz) tomato
  passata
2 sprigs of fresh thyme

Preheat the oven to 220°C/Fan 200°C/Gas 7. You will need an ovenproof dish about 20 × 28 × 5cm (8 × 11 × 2 in), with a capacity of about 1.7 litres (3 pints).

**1** First cut the aubergines in half, score them and sprinkle the cut side with a little salt. Leave for about 15 minutes then squeeze to remove the salty juices.

**2** Boil the potatoes until not quite done, for about 15–20 minutes, in salted water. Allow to cool enough to handle, then skin and cut in half.

**3** Toss the aubergines, onions, whole garlic cloves and peppers in a couple of tablespoons of olive oil and season well. Arrange cut sides down on a large shallow baking sheet or roasting tin. Roast in the preheated oven until the peppers are charred and the vegetables are soft, about 20–30 minutes, turning once. You may find the peppers take longest, therefore remove the other vegetables, keeping them in separate piles.

**4** When the peppers are charred and hot, transfer them to a polythene bag, seal the top and let them sweat and cool in the bag. When cold, peel off the skin.

*Recipe continued overleaf*

### COOK NOW EAT LATER

### TO PREPARE AHEAD
Prepare to the end of step 6. Cool, and keep in the fridge for up to 2 days. Cook as in step 7, about 15–20 minutes.

### TO FREEZE
Freeze at the end of step 6. Defrost thoroughly, then cook as in step 7, for about 15–20 minutes.

**COOK NOW EAT LATER**

## TO COOK IN THE AGA
Cook step 3 on the second set of runners in the Roasting Oven for about 20–30 minutes. Cook step 7 directly on the floor of the Roasting Oven for about 15 minutes then slide on to the second set of runners for a further 10 minutes.

## TIP
Large onions of the Spanish sort have a tough layer of skin directly under the brown skin. It's best to peel this second skin off before using in recipes otherwise it will never soften down, even after long, slow cooking.

*Recipe continued*

**5** Slice the aubergines into 5mm (¼ in) slices, and cut the peppers into chunky pieces. Squash the garlic with the back of a knife and add the soft flesh to the peppers.

Turn the oven down to 200°C/Fan 180°C/Gas 6.

**6** Arrange the vegetables in layers in the dish. Layer the potato with seasoning, rosemary and about 6 tablespoons of passata, followed by onion, pepper and aubergine, still with herbs and passata in between each layer. Push in the sprigs of thyme near the top (these need to be removed to serve).

**7** Cook in the hot oven for about 15 minutes (or a lower temperature for longer if it suits you). Remove the sprigs of thyme to serve.

# Aromatic Thai Rice

This is delicious, and good with many oriental meat and fish dishes.
Use any quick-cook rice as I find this far easier to get light separate
grains than with white Thai rice. Use a good chicken stock
if you are not vegetarian.

**COOK NOW EAT LATER**

**TO PREPARE AHEAD**
Cook the rice then turn
into a bowl, cool rapidly
and keep in the fridge
for up to 6 hours. To
reheat, place the rice
on a large sheet of
buttered foil and
sprinkle with a little
water. Wrap in a neat,
tightly sealed parcel
and bake in the oven
preheated to 150°C/Fan
130°C/Gas 2 for about
25–30 minutes until
piping hot.

**TO FREEZE**
Not suitable.

**TO COOK IN THE AGA**
Bring the rice to the
boil on the Boiling
Plate, stir, cover
and transfer to the
Simmering Oven for
about 15–20 minutes
or until all the liquid
has been absorbed.

3 tablespoons sunflower oil
1 medium onion, chopped
1 red chilli, seeded and
    finely chopped
1 fat garlic clove, crushed
1 teaspoon garam masala
350g (12 oz) long grain
    white rice

1 lemongrass bulb,
    crushed lightly
    with a rolling pin
1 good teaspoon salt
500ml (18 fl oz)
    vegetable stock
½ lime
chopped fresh coriander

**1** Heat the oil in a heavy-based pan, add the onion
and cook for a few minutes until starting to soften.

**2** Add the chilli, garlic, garam masala, rice, lemongrass
and salt, and stir.

**3** Pour in the stock and add the half lime in one piece.
Bring to the boil, stir, cover and simmer very gently
for about 10 minutes, or until all the liquid has been
absorbed. Remove the lemongrass and lime, having
squeezed out any juice.

**4** Serve immediately garnished with fresh coriander.

# Herbed Fondant Potatoes

A classic dish, cooking the potatoes simply in butter. Chefs always 'turn' their potatoes into a pretty ridged shape, but I think life is too short for that, so we have sliced them! Do be careful when turning them over so as not to break them up. The potatoes should not be brown, they should be pale in colour.

**TO PREPARE AHEAD**
Cook to the end of step 1, arrange in the ovenproof dish and put in the fridge up to 12 hours ahead. To reheat, bring to room temperature and then continue with steps 2 and 3.

**TO FREEZE**
Not suitable.

**TO COOK IN THE AGA**
Cook step 1 on the Simmering Plate for about 10 minutes. Arrange in overlapping slices in an ovenproof dish, cover with foil and put on the grid shelf on the floor of the Roasting Oven for about 10 minutes. Transfer to the Simmering Oven for a further 1½ hours.

1kg (2¼ lb) large King Edward potatoes, peeled
50g (2 oz) butter
salt and freshly ground black pepper

1 tablespoon snipped fresh chives
1 tablespoon chopped fresh parsley

Preheat the oven to 160°C/Fan 140°C/Gas 3.

**1** Cut the peeled potatoes into 5mm (¼ in) slices. Melt the butter in a deep non-stick saucepan or casserole dish. Add the potatoes and turn over so they are all coated in the melted butter. Season with salt and pepper, cover with a lid and simmer over a low heat for about 15 minutes.

**2** Remove from the heat and cool slightly. Arrange the slices in a shallow 1.2 litre (2 pint) ovenproof dish (no need to butter) so they are overlapping each other. Cover with foil and bake in the preheated oven for about 1½ hours until the potatoes are tender but not coloured.

**3** Just before serving, sprinkle over the herbs, pushing them between the layers.

# Mash Crazy!

Mash is one of the world's favourite potato dishes, so we thought we'd give you a choice! Remember to think of the dishes you are serving the mash with, to ensure the flavours complement each other.

Boil peeled cubed potatoes in boiling salted water until tender. Drain, add milk and butter, salt and pepper, and mash until mixed, then beat with a hand whisk until smooth and creamy. Choose from the list below and stir in at the end to make the mash extra special! For each 1kg (2¼ lb) potatoes – to serve 4–6 – add:

## Grainy Mustard Mash
about 3 tablespoons grainy mustard

## Creamy Horseradish Mash
about 4–5 tablespoons creamed horseradish

## Mediterranean Mash
about 2 tablespoons olive oil
50g (2 oz) chopped black olives
8 sun-dried tomatoes, chopped

## Fresh Herb and Garlic Mash
a small bunch chopped fresh parsley
a small bunch snipped chives
2 fat garlic cloves, crushed

## Mature Cheddar Mash
about 75g (3 oz) mature Cheddar, coarsely grated

## Red or Green Pesto Mash
about 3 tablespoons red or green pesto

COOK NOW
EAT LATER

**TO PREPARE AHEAD**
Mashed potato is best served straightaway, but if you wish to do it some hours ahead, quickly cool the mash and check the seasoning. Well butter a shallow ovenproof dish large enough to give a layer of mashed potato that is 5cm (2 in) deep. Roughly fork over the top and add a few knobs of butter. Blast in a very hot oven at 220°C/Fan 200°C/Gas 7 for about 20 minutes and serve immediately.

**TO FREEZE**
Not suitable.

**TO COOK IN THE AGA**
If reheating the mash in the dish, do so on the top set of runners in the Roasting Oven.

COOK NOW, EAT LATER

✻

# Hot
# Puddings

**CHAPTER SEVEN**

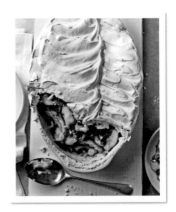

Few people these days think of serving a hot pudding, and excuses range from 'it takes too much time' and 'it's complicated' to 'it's fattening'... But the truth is that none of these is strictly true. Sweet things are generally considered to be more calorific, but most of the puddings here are based on fruit, and add a healthy touch at the end of a meal. And if you are really worried about your weight, simply have a smaller helping and say no to the accompanying cream (that's where most calories lie).

And it's not true to say that hot puddings are more complicated to cook. A novice cook could quickly master something like the caramelised peaches. But the best news about these hot puddings is that they are so quick to make. All can be prepared well in advance, and then baked just before serving (some can even be baked ahead and reheated). What could be easier than putting your hot pudding into the oven as you finish serving the main course? And most of the puddings here even save you time on the washing-up: they are served from the dish in which they are cooked.

Serve hot puddings with a cold pouring cream or a dollop of low-fat crème fraîche, rather than double cream (not so rich). And remember that if you heat crème fraîche or soured cream, they become the consistency of milk – not what you want for this purpose. Always serve them cold.

# Pear Tarte Tatin

You can of course use apples instead. Do not use a loose-bottomed
tin as the liquid will run out of the bottom!

**COOK NOW EAT LATER**

### TO PREPARE AHEAD
Step 1 can be completed
up to 2 days ahead. The
tart can be completely
made up to 8 hours
ahead. Drain off the
juices while hot and
boil to thicken just
before serving. Reheat
the tart in a hot oven at
200°C/Fan 180°C/Gas
6 for 15 minutes. Cover
if getting too brown.
Turn out and pour the
thickened sauce over.

### TO FREEZE
Not suitable.

### TO COOK IN THE AGA
Cook the assembled
tart on the grid shelf
on the floor of the
Roasting Oven for
about 40 minutes. Slide
the cold sheet on to the
second set of runners
after 10 minutes if
getting too brown.

100g (4 oz) butter
100g (4 oz) muscovado sugar
900g–1.1kg (2–2½ lb) pears,
   ripe but firm

1 × 500g packet
   puff pastry
icing sugar for dusting

Line a 20cm (8 in) round deep cake tin with a fixed base,
(7.5cm/3 in deep) with a circle of non-stick baking paper.
Preheat the oven to 220°C/Fan 200°C/Gas 7.

**1** Gently heat the butter and sugar together in a small
pan until both have melted and the mixture is smooth
and a golden straw colour. Pour into the prepared cake
tin and spread out evenly with the back of a wet spoon
to cover the base of the tin. You may not need to do this:
it may just run over the base by itself.

**2** Peel, core and slice the pears, about 5mm (¼ in) thick.
Arrange in overlapping circles on top of the sugar
mixture to use all of the pears. They will come right
to the top of the tin.

**3** Roll out the pastry on a lightly floured work surface
so that it is just larger than the diameter of the cake tin.
Place the pastry over the pears and push the pastry
edges down into the tin to neaten. Make a small cross
in the top of the pastry to let the steam out.

**4** Bake in the preheated oven for about 40 minutes until
the pastry is a good golden brown. Allow to cool for about
10 minutes. Leaving the tart in the tin, carefully tip the
tin to drain off the juice. Boil up the juices in a small pan
until a pouring consistency.

**5** Carefully invert the tart on to a heatproof serving
plate. Pour the thickened juices over the tart and dust
with icing sugar. Serve warm with Greek yoghurt or
crème fraîche.

# Toffee Apple Puddings
## with Toffee Sauce

Deliciously naughty puddings, which are very quick and easy, and can be made in moulds (available from good kitchen shops and by mail order), and baked later. There may be too much toffee sauce for you, but it keeps in the fridge for 1 month and is excellent over ice cream.

**TO PREPARE AHEAD**

Prepare the sauce up to 3 days ahead. Reheat gently in a saucepan to serve. Prepare to the end of step 2 up to 24 hours ahead. Keep the unbaked puddings chilled until ready to bake, but they will take a little longer to cook from cold. They can also be baked and kept warm, still in the moulds, in a low oven at 140°C/Fan 120°C/Gas 1 for up to 40 minutes, still covered with foil.

**TO FREEZE**

Not suitable.

100g (4 oz) butter or baking margarine, at room temperature
50g (2 oz) light muscovado sugar
1 tablespoon golden syrup
2 eggs
150g (5 oz) self-raising flour
1 level teaspoon baking powder

**Topping**
200g (7 oz) butter
200g (7 oz) light muscovado sugar
juice of ½ lemon
2–3 dessert apples, peeled, cored and chopped into sultana-sized pieces

**Toffee Sauce**
50g (2 oz) butter
150g (5 oz) light muscovado sugar
150g (5 oz) golden syrup
1 × 170g can evaporated milk
juice of ½ lemon (optional)

Lightly grease the insides of 8 × 150ml (¼ pint) pudding moulds. Preheat the oven to 220°C/Fan 200°C/Gas 7.

**1** First make the topping. Melt the butter and sugar together in a small pan over a gentle heat, add the lemon juice and apples, and divide between the pudding moulds.

**2** Measure the pudding ingredients (not including the sauce ingredients) into a food processor and mix until blended, scraping down the sides of the bowl once. (Be careful not to over-beat.) Or mix the ingredients in a bowl with an electric hand-held whisk. Spoon the mixture on to the apples in the pudding moulds: two-thirds fill each one. Cover each mould with a square of buttered foil.

**3** Line a small roasting tin (the right size to fit the 8 pudding moulds comfortably) with a piece of kitchen paper, put in the moulds and half fill the tin with boiling water. Cover completely with foil and bake in the preheated oven for 30–35 minutes until the puddings are well risen and firm to the touch.

**4** Meanwhile, make the sauce. Measure the butter, sugar and syrup into a pan, and heat gently until melted and liquid. Gently boil for 5 minutes. Remove from the heat and gradually add the evaporated milk. The sauce is now ready. Leave on one side and heat to piping hot to serve. If you find the sauce too sweet, add lemon juice to taste.

**5** When the puddings are ready, remove from the oven, loosen the sides, and turn out. Serve drizzled with hot toffee sauce.

**TO COOK IN THE AGA**
At step 3, slide the roasting tin, half filled with hot water and covered with foil, directly on to the floor of the Roasting Oven for about 15 minutes. Turn once and continue to bake for a further 15 minutes until well risen and firm to the touch. Keep warm in the moulds for up to 40 minutes in the roasting tin in the Simmering Oven, still covered with foil.

**TIP**
If cooking in ramekins, line the base of the roasting tin with a piece of kitchen paper as this stops the ramekins sliding about. If using an aluminium tin, put a wedge of lemon in the water, as this prevents a black line appearing.

# Caramelised Peaches
## with Brandy

The peaches can also be left whole for this recipe,
if they look particularly tempting and delicious.

6 fresh peaches or nectarines    ground cinnamon
soft butter    brandy
demerara sugar

Preheat the oven to 200°C/Fan 180°C/Gas 6.

**1** Peel the peaches or nectarines by dipping into boiling
water until the skin is easy to remove (as you would
skin a tomato). Cut in half and remove the stones.
Dry with kitchen paper, then rub the rounded side
of each peach or nectarine with soft butter.

**2** Pack the peaches or nectarines cut side down into
a dish in which they fit tightly. Sprinkle with demerara
sugar and cinnamon and pour about 6 tablespoons
of brandy into the dish around them.

**3** Bake in the preheated oven for about 30 minutes
until tender.

**4** Serve hot with crème fraîche or cream.

## TO PREPARE AHEAD
Cook up to 12 hours
ahead of time, but only
for 20 minutes. Cover
and store in a cool place
for up to 12 hours.
Reheat in a hot oven
at 200°C/Fan 180 °C/
Gas 6 for about 10–15
minutes. Sprinkle with
a little more demerara
sugar first.

## TO FREEZE
Not suitable.

## TO COOK IN THE AGA
Bake on the top set
of runners in the
Roasting Oven for
about 15 minutes until
the fruit is tender.

# Cherry Queen of Puddings

If preferred, use raspberry jam, but I think cherry is best.
You could also use mincemeat at Christmas.

600ml (1 pint) milk
25g (1 oz) butter
finely grated zest of 1 lemon
225g (8 oz) caster sugar
3 eggs, separated

75g (3 oz) fresh fine white
    breadcrumbs
4–5 good tablespoons cherry
    jam, warmed

Preheat the oven to 160°C/Fan 140°C/Gas 3 and grease
a 1.25 litre (2 pint) shallow (about 5cm/2 in) ovenproof
dish, one that will fit flat in a roasting tin.

**1** To start the custard base, very gently warm the milk
in a small saucepan. Add the butter, lemon zest and
50g (2 oz) of the sugar, and stir until dissolved.

**2** Lightly whisk the egg yolks in a bowl and gradually
pour and whisk in the warmed milk.

**3** Sprinkle the breadcrumbs over the base of the buttered
dish and pour in the custard. Leave to stand for about
15 minutes for the breadcrumbs to absorb the liquid.

**4** Carefully transfer the dish to a roasting tin and fill
the tin halfway with boiling water. Bake in the preheated
oven for about 25–30 minutes until the custard has set.

**5** Whisk the egg whites on maximum speed in an electric
mixer. When stiff, add the remaining sugar, 1 teaspoon
at a time (whisking on maximum speed) until stiff
and shiny.

**6** Remove the custard from the oven and turn the
temperature down to 150°C/Fan 130°C/Gas 2. Pour the
warm jam over the custard and then spread the meringue
over the top. Arrange the top in rough peaks. Return
to the oven and bake for about 25–30 minutes until the
meringue is pale golden all over and crisp. Serve at once
with cream.

### TO PREPARE AHEAD
Bake the custard base,
and spread with the
cherry jam up to 24
hours ahead. Keep in
the fridge. Whisk and
bake the meringue to
serve (the cooking time
may be a little longer).

### TO FREEZE
Not suitable.

### TO COOK IN THE AGA
Bake the custard on
the grid shelf on the
floor of the Roasting
Oven with the cold shelf
on the second set of
runners for about 20
minutes. Transfer to
the Simmering Oven
for about 15 minutes
or until set. At step 6,
return to the Roasting
Oven on the grid shelf
on the floor with the
cold shelf on the second
set of runners, for about
8 minutes, turning after
4 minutes, then transfer
to the Simmering Oven
for about 10 minutes
until crisp.

# Easy Lime and Lemon Meringue Pie

This delicious recipe is a bit of a cheat, as we are not making a classic lemon curd. Instead, we're using condensed milk. The base is a crumb crust without sugar as the filling is on the sweet side. Once made and baked, it is best eaten on the same day.

**COOK NOW EAT LATER**

### TO PREPARE AHEAD
The flan dish can be lined with the biscuit crumb mix, covered and kept in the fridge for up to 3 days. The filling can be mixed, covered and kept in the fridge for up to 8 hours before baking. Once baked, the pie can be eaten warm or cold, but the meringue shrinks a little on standing.

### TO FREEZE
Not suitable.

**Base**
75g (3 oz) butter
175g (6 oz) digestive biscuits, crushed

**Filling**
1 × 394g can sweetened condensed milk
3 egg yolks
finely grated zest and juice of 2 limes and 2 large lemons

**Topping**
3 egg whites
175g (6 oz) caster sugar

You will need a 23cm (9 in) fluted china flan dish, or a shallow, straight-sided round dish about 4cm (1½ in) deep. Preheat the oven to 190°C/Fan 170°C/Gas 5.

**1** For the base, melt the butter in a medium-sized pan. Remove the pan from the heat and stir in the biscuit crumbs. Press the mixture into the flan dish using the back of a spoon to bring the crumbs up round the edge of the dish and smooth the base evenly.

**2** For the filling, pour the condensed milk into a bowl, then beat in the egg yolks, lemon and lime zest and strained juices. The mixture will seem to thicken slightly on standing, then loosen again as soon as it is stirred. This is caused by the combination of condensed milk and citrus juices and is nothing to worry about. Pour the mixture into the biscuit-lined dish.

**3** For the topping, measure the egg whites into a large, grease-free bowl and, preferably using an electric hand whisk (or otherwise a balloon whisk), whisk the egg whites until stiff but not dry. Now start adding the sugar slowly, 1 teaspoon at a time, whisking well between each addition at full speed. When about two-thirds of the sugar has been added, the process can be speeded up. In total it should take about 8 minutes (2–3 minutes with one of the latest free-standing mixers).

**4** Pile separate spoons of meringue over the surface of the filling, then spread gently to cover the filling to the biscuit edge. Lightly swirl the meringue to finish.

**5** Bake in the preheated oven for about 15–20 minutes or until the meringue is pale golden. The meringue should be soft inside and a little crisp on top. Leave aside for about 30 minutes before serving warm. This will give the filling time to firm up a little and therefore make serving easier.

**TO COOK IN THE AGA**
Bake on the grid shelf of the Roasting Oven on the third set of runners for about 2–3 minutes until a pale golden colour, then transfer to the centre of the Simmering Oven for a further 15 minutes or so.

# Saucy Chocolate and Walnut Pudding

This is a classic recipe but usually made with lemon. The sponge goes on the bottom and the sauce is poured over the top: when cooked the sponge has risen and the sauce is at the bottom. If you are not keen on walnuts, leave them out, or replace with chocolate chips.

**COOK NOW EAT LATER**

### TO PREPARE AHEAD
Make the sponge mixture and sauce up to 4 hours ahead, but keep separately, the sponge in its buttered dish and the sauce in its bowl. Spoon the sauce over the sponge just before baking.

### TO FREEZE
Not suitable.

### TO COOK IN THE AGA
Slide the pudding dish on to the lowest set of runners in the Roasting Oven for about 10 minutes. Slide the cold sheet on to the second set of runners for a further 10 minutes or so until the pudding is springy to touch and a dark chocolate brown.

50g (2 oz) butter, melted, plus extra for greasing
4 eggs
100g (4 oz) caster sugar
½ teaspoon vanilla extract
100g (4 oz) self-raising flour
50g (2 oz) cocoa powder
2 teaspoons baking powder
50g (2 oz) shelled walnuts or pecans, coarsely chopped
icing sugar for sprinkling

**Sauce**
100g (4 oz) light muscovado sugar
3 tablespoons cocoa powder
450ml (¾ pint) boiling water

Lightly butter an ovenproof dish, 1.4 litre (2 pint) in capacity and 9cm (3½ in) deep. Preheat the oven to 180°C/Fan 160°C/Gas 4.

**1** Whisk together the eggs, caster sugar and vanilla extract until well blended. Pour the melted butter on to the eggs and then sift in the flour, cocoa powder and baking powder. Mix thoroughly then stir in the walnuts or pecans. Pour the mixture into the buttered dish.

**2** To make the sauce, sift the muscovado sugar and cocoa powder into a medium bowl and gradually whisk in the boiling water. Cool slightly, then pour the sauce over the pudding mixture.

**3** Bake in the preheated oven for about 30–40 minutes until the sauce has sunk to the bottom and the sponge is well risen, springy to the touch and a dark chocolate brown.

**4** Sprinkle with icing sugar and serve immediately with cream, crème fraîche, custard, ice cream, or all four!

# Rhubarb Oaty Crumble

Classic crumble with oats in the topping. Depending on how young your rhubarb is, you may need to add a little more sugar.

**Filling**
10 sticks (about 750g/1¾ lb)
   young pink rhubarb sticks
75g (3 oz) soft brown sugar
2 tablespoons water

**Crumble Topping**
150g (5 oz) plain flour
75g (3 oz) porridge oats
100g (4 oz) butter
75g (3 oz) caster sugar

Preheat the oven to 200°C/Fan 180°C /Gas 6. You will need a 30 × 23 × 5cm (12 × 9 × 2 in) ovenproof dish (1.7 litre/3 pint).

**1** Cut the rhubarb sticks into 5cm (2 in) pieces and arrange in the bottom of the dish. Sprinkle over the sugar and toss to mix, and then pour over the water.

**2** For the topping, place the ingredients in a bowl and rub with your fingertips until it looks the consistency of breadcrumbs. Sprinkle over the rhubarb in the dish, completely covering it.

**3** Transfer to the preheated oven and cook for 50 minutes, or until pale golden and bubbling around the edges.

**4** Serve warm with cream, ice cream or custard.

**COOK NOW EAT LATER**

**TO PREPARE AHEAD**
Complete to the end of step 2 up to 12 hours ahead, cover with clingfilm and leave in the fridge. Continue with step 3.

**TO FREEZE**
Not suitable.

**TO COOK IN THE AGA**
Bake on the top set of runners in the Roasting Oven for 50 minutes.

# Chocolate and Vanilla Marbled Puddings

These are quick and easy to make and perfect for the family. We use 150ml (¼ pint) timbale moulds, but you could use ramekins if you prefer.

**COOK NOW EAT LATER**

**TO PREPARE AHEAD**
Can be made up to a day ahead and reheated gently in a moderate oven to serve.

**TO FREEZE**
Not suitable.

**TO COOK IN THE AGA**
Bake on the grid shelf on the floor of the roasting oven for 25 minutes or until risen.

175g (6 oz) softened butter
175g (6 oz) caster sugar
175g (6 oz) self-raising flour
3 large eggs
½ teaspoon baking powder

1 ½ tablespoons cocoa powder, blended with 2 tablespoons boiling water
2 teaspoons vanilla extract

Preheat the oven to 180°C/Fan 160°C /Gas 4. You will need 6 × 150ml (¼ pint) pudding basins, buttered and base-lined with a disc of baking parchment.

**1** Measure the butter, sugar, flour, eggs and baking powder into a bowl and mix with an electric hand whisk until combined.

**2** Divide the mixture into 2 equal halves. Add the blended cocoa to one half and the vanilla extract to the other half.

**3** Spoon alternate teaspoonfuls of the mixture into the pudding basins and then swirl with a skewer – right down to the bottom of the basins.

**4** Cover each pudding with a square of buttered, pleated foil.

**5** Place on a baking sheet and bake in the preheated oven for 30 minutes, or until risen and springy to the touch. Leave for 5 minutes and then run a knife around the edge to loosen and turn out on to a plate.

**6** Serve warm with Chocolatey Chocolate Sauce (page 205).

# Chocolatey Chocolate Sauce

The quickest, easiest sauce which goes incredibly well with ice cream, desserts, sponges, fresh fruit – anything, in fact!

175g (6 oz) plain chocolate (39 per cent cocoa solids)

1 × 170g can evaporated milk

**COOK NOW EAT LATER**

**1** Break the chocolate into cubes.

**2** Pour the milk into a small non-stick saucepan and stir over a medium heat until just below boiling point.

**3** Remove from the heat and immediately add the chopped chocolate and stir until melted and smooth.

**4** Serve over vanilla ice cream, Walnut Praline Parfait (page 214), Chocolate and Vanilla Marbled Puddings (page 202), or anything you fancy.

**TO PREPARE AHEAD**
Can be made up to 3 days ahead and gently reheated in a pan to serve.

**TO FREEZE**
Not suitable.

**TO COOK IN THE AGA**
Heat the milk gently on the simmering plate and continue as step 3.

# Apple Mincemeat Alaska

This is a very quick and easy pudding, best served warm with cream.
Use the spare egg yolks to make fresh lemon curd (see page 222).

**COOK NOW EAT LATER**

**TO PREPARE AHEAD**
Prepare step 1 up
to 6 hours ahead.

**TO FREEZE**
Not suitable.

**TO COOK IN THE AGA**
Bring the apples to
heat on the Boiling
Plate, then cover
and transfer to the
Simmering Oven for
about 30 minutes
until the apples are
tender. At step 5, slide
the dish on to the grid
shelf on the floor of
the Roasting Oven
for about 4 minutes
until pale golden
brown. Transfer
to the Simmering
Oven for a further
30 minutes until the
meringue is crisp.

900g (2 1b) cooking apples,
   peeled and cored,
   thickly sliced
25g (1 oz) butter
juice and zest of ½ lemon
8 trifle sponges, about
   175g (6 oz)
1 × 400g jar good-quality
   mincemeat
4 tablespoons brandy
   or Calvados

**Meringue**
3 large egg whites
175g (6 oz) caster sugar

Butter a 20–23cm (8–9 in) round, shallow china ovenproof
dish. Preheat the oven to 180°C/Fan 160°C/Gas 4.

**1** Thickly slice the apples into a shallow saucepan with
the butter, lemon juice and zest. Heat gently until the
butter has melted, then cover and simmer gently for
about 15–20 minutes until the apples are tender. Allow
to cool slightly.

**2** Arrange the trifle sponges evenly over the base of the
dish, cutting to fit.

**3** Whisk the egg whites for the meringue in a large clean
bowl with an electric hand whisk on full speed until stiff.
Gradually add the sugar, 1 teaspoon at a time, whisking
continuously, still on full speed, until the mixture is stiff
and glossy.

**4** Mix the mincemeat and brandy or Calvados with
the apples and spread over the trifle sponges. Spoon the
meringue mixture on top and spread out evenly, covering
all the mincemeat and apples so no holes appear.

**5** Bake in the preheated oven for about 20–25 minutes,
watching carefully, until the meringue is crisp and
a pale golden brown. Serve immediately.

# Raspberry Frangipane Tarts

Delicious and easy individual tarts – raspberry and almond is a lovely combination.

## TO PREPARE AHEAD
The pastry-lined flan tin can be kept, covered with clingfilm, in the fridge for up to 12 hours. Filled with the jam and almond filling, it can be kept for about 1 hour, covered and refrigerated.

## TO FREEZE
You can freeze the tarts, once baked and before glazing, for up to 1 month.

## TO COOK IN THE AGA
Bake directly on the floor of the Roasting Oven for 15 minutes.

**Pastry**
225g (8 oz) plain flour
100g (4 oz) butter, cubed
50g (2 oz) icing sugar
1 egg
1 tablespoon water

**Almond Filling**
175g (6 oz) softened butter
175g (6 oz) caster sugar
4 eggs
175g (6 oz) ground almonds
1 teaspoon almond extract
125g (4½ oz) raspberry jam

**To Finish**
100g (4 oz) icing sugar
about 1 tablespoon water
175g (6 oz) fresh raspberries

Preheat the oven to 200°C/Fan 180 °C/Gas 6, and put a heavy, flat baking tray inside to heat up. You will need 2 × 4-hole Yorkshire pudding tins.

**1** Make the pastry, either by the rubbing-in method or measure the flour and butter into a processor and process. Add the sugar and mix for a moment, then add the egg and water. Process until the mixture just holds together (you may need a dash more water). Remove the pastry.

**2** To make the almond filling, place the butter and sugar in the processor and process until creamy. Add the eggs and blend, then add the ground almonds and almond extract.

**3** Divide the pastry into eight. Roll each piece into a circle and then use a 12cm (4½ in) cutter to make a neat circle. Line each hole with pastry and prick the base of each one with a fork. Spread the jam evenly over each base of pastry and divide the almond mixture between the pastry cases.

**4** Sit the trays on the hot baking sheet, and bake in the preheated oven for about 20 minutes, until the pastry is crisp and the filling is golden brown.

**5** To finish the tart, make a glacé icing from the icing sugar and water, mixing until it is a pouring consistency. Drizzle each tart with the icing in a zig-zag pattern and arrange a few raspberries over the top.

COOK NOW, EAT LATER

✦

# Cold
# Desserts

CHAPTER EIGHT

Every single recipe in this chapter can be made in advance – at least the day before – and indeed the majority can be frozen. This is exactly why cold desserts are so popular. Once you have a tray of mousses or a bowl of fruit salad in the fridge, or an ice cream in the freezer, you can forget completely about one course of your meal and concentrate on the others.

The ice creams are delicious and made from a whipped meringue and whipped cream mixture, so the volume is there before they are frozen. This means that they do not need any re-whisking, which saves time and energy. However, they do contain raw egg, so be aware when serving to the very young, the elderly or to pregnant ladies.

You can go to town serving cold desserts, and I love decorating the plates. My icing sugar sifter works well, especially over the chocolate terrine, and I always have a spray of berries or currants if the dessert is fruit based. A good tip when serving ice cream is to scoop it out into balls in advance and place back in the freezer, covered with clingfilm. This makes serving much easier – just remember to remove from the freezer 10 minutes or so in advance so they come to eating temperature and texture.

A final thought. If you are serving two desserts, make sure they are quite different: one rich, gooey and calorific, the other something like a fruit salad or a sorbet. People can then choose what they like – one or the other, or indeed both!

# Double Chocolate Terrine

Serve in thinnish slices as it is very naughty! Make the terrine
1 day ahead so that it's really firm.

## COOK NOW EAT LATER

**TO PREPARE AHEAD**
This can be made up
to 2 days ahead. Make
completely and turn
out, leaving the
clingfilm intact. Peel
off and decorate before
serving straight from
the fridge.

**TO FREEZE**
Once set, turn out,
wrap in a second layer
of clingfilm and freeze
for up to 1 month.
Thaw for about 6 hours.

**TO COOK IN THE AGA**
Melt the chocolates
in separate bowls
on a tea-towel at
the back of the Aga
several hours ahead.

**TIP**
Decorate the terrine
with shavings of dark
chocolate – this is very
easy to do with a potato
peeler and it gives
a lovely effect.

**White Chocolate Layer**
200g (7 oz) 100% Belgium
    white chocolate
1 × 200g tub full-fat Italian
    mascarpone cheese

**Dark Chocolate Layers**
350g (12 oz) plain chocolate
    (39 per cent cocoa solids),
    plus extra for decorating
450ml (¾ pint) double cream
2 egg yolks
2 tablespoons brandy

Line a 900g (2 lb) loaf tin with clingfilm.

**1** For the white chocolate layer, break the chocolate into
a bowl and carefully melt over a pan of hot water. Don't let
the chocolate become too hot or it will go grainy; it should
be slightly hotter than lukewarm. Stir in the mascarpone
and mix until smooth (you may need a whisk to get it
really smooth). Leave to cool.

**2** For the dark chocolate layers, break the chocolate into
a food processor and process to a fine powder. Heat half
of the cream to just below boiling point and pour this in.
Process until smooth, then add the egg yolks and brandy.
Mix until blended. Whisk the remaining cream in a bowl
to soft peaks and fold into the dark chocolate mixture.

**3** Pour some of the dark chocolate mixture to reach
one-third of the way up the lined tin, then transfer to the
freezer for about 1 hour, until set. When just set, pour in
the white chocolate and freeze for about 2 hours until set.
Spoon the remaining dark chocolate on top of the white
chocolate mixture, cover and put back into the freezer
for about 6 hours until firm or simply leave in the fridge
overnight to set.

**4** To serve, you may want to freeze the terrine for about
30 minutes, which makes cutting easier. Remove the
clingfilm and serve in slices (it helps to cut the terrine
with a hot knife).

# Walnut Praline Parfait

A very easy and delicious dessert, generously given to me by Vicky, a close neighbour. Just take it out of the freezer about 10 minutes before serving – what could be easier!

### TO PREPARE AHEAD

Prepare and freeze up to 1 month ahead. In which case, forget the reserved praline and simply sprinkle with icing sugar and some fresh mint to serve.

### TO COOK IN THE AGA

Dissolve the sugar for the praline on the Simmering Plate, discard the spoon, then transfer to the Boiling Plate, and boil until a light caramel colour.

4 eggs, separated
100g (4 oz) caster sugar
300ml (½ pint) pouring double cream
1 teaspoon vanilla extract

**Praline**
100g (4 oz) caster sugar
6 tablespoons water
100g (4 oz) walnut pieces

You will need 8 ramekins.

**1** To make the praline, dissolve the sugar and water in a small saucepan (not non-stick), stirring until all the sugar is dissolved. Turn up the heat, discard the spoon, and boil until a light caramel colour. Stir in the walnuts and pour on to non-stick paper for the praline to set. Once the praline is cold, chop into small sultana-sized pieces.

**2** Whisk the egg whites in a mixer, or with an electric hand whisk on maximum speed, until stiff. Gradually add the sugar 1 teaspoon at a time until well incorporated and the mixture is stiff and glossy. Fold in the egg yolks.

**3** Whisk the cream with the vanilla extract until just thick. Fold into the egg mixture, along with most of the chopped praline (reserve a little for garnish).

**4** Pour into 8 ramekins, cover with clingfilm and freeze for a minimum of 12 hours.

**5** Remove the parfait from the freezer about 10 minutes before serving and top with the reserved praline.

# Quite the Best Summer Pudding

This summer pudding is all fruit and very little bread. I make it fairly shallow in a straight-sided soufflé dish or glass dish. The shallowness means that even though there is much more fruit than bread, the pudding doesn't collapse when turned out. There will be fruit left, so serve it with the pudding, which should be really well chilled.

**COOK NOW EAT LATER**

**TO PREPARE AHEAD**
Make up to 2 days ahead and keep in the fridge.

**TO FREEZE**
Cover and freeze at the end of step 2. Thaw overnight at room temperature. The pudding will be quite soft after freezing.

**TO COOK IN THE AGA**
Bring the fruits to the boil on the Boiling Plate, cover and transfer to the Simmering Oven for about 15 minutes, or until the fruits are just tender.

350g (12 oz) blackberries
350g (12 oz) blackcurrants
350g (12 oz) redcurrants
1 small punnet, about 150g
   (5 oz) blueberries,
   if available

350g (12 oz) caster sugar
225g (8 oz) raspberries
8 slices thin sliced bread,
   crusts removed
pouring cream to serve

You will need a 1.1 litre (2 pint) soufflé dish or straight-sided dish, 15 × 8cm (6 × 3 in).

**1** Measure all the fruits except the raspberries into a pan with a tablespoon of water. Add the sugar and bring to the boil, then gently simmer until the fruits are just tender. Cool a little, then add the raspberries.

**2** Cut the bread to shapes to fit the base and sides of the dish to about 5cm (2 in) up the side. Dip the bread into the juice first then line the dish, putting the fruit-soaked side nearest the dish. Fill the dish just under half full with some of the fruit, then put a layer of bread over the fruit. Add more fruit on top and finally the last slices of bread, spooning a little of the juice over the bread at the top. You should have about 200ml (7 fl oz) of fruit left over to serve with the pudding. Put a small plate on top, press down lightly, then cover with clingfilm and refrigerate overnight.

**3** Turn out into a shallow dish a little larger than the summer pudding, so that the juices are caught. I serve it with extra reserved fruit and pouring cream.

# Divine Lemon Pots

Probably the easiest dessert you will ever make – and so delicious too! It came my way from a dear friend Di. Four of us play tennis every Monday and often swap recipes and ideas over coffee. It has become a firm favourite ever since.

600ml (1 pint) pouring
   double cream
150g (5 oz) caster sugar

finely grated zest and
   juice of 3 lemons
16 fresh raspberries

You will need 8 small coffee cups, wine glasses or tiny ramekins.

**1** Heat the cream, sugar and lemon zest in a wide-based pan over a low heat until at simmering point. Stir continuously for about 3 minutes.

**2** Remove from the heat and allow to cool slightly (until lukewarm).

**3** Mix the lemon juice with the cooled cream and sugar, and stir.

**4** Pour the lemon cream into the cups. Transfer to the fridge to set for a minimum of 2 hours.

**5** To serve, arrange 2 raspberries on top of each pot when the cream has set.

**COOK NOW
EAT LATER**

**TO PREPARE AHEAD**
These can be made up to 24 hours before serving, and kept in the fridge.

**TO FREEZE**
Not suitable.

**TO COOK IN THE AGA**
Cook step 1 on the Simmering Plate.

# Eton Mess
## with Lemon Curd and Raspberries

SERVES 8

One of my favourite desserts, quick and easy to make and, if you do not want to make meringues, it is a perfect recipe for using up leftover ones. If so you will need 100g (4 oz) of cooked meringue.

**COOK NOW EAT LATER**

### TO PREPARE AHEAD
Best to make and serve the dessert within 2 hours of mixing together. Keep in a cool place but not the fridge, otherwise the moisture softens the meringues too much and makes them runny. You can keep meringues in a plastic bag in a cold place for up to 2 months.

### TO FREEZE
Not suitable.

### TO COOK IN THE AGA
Bake the meringue in the Simmering Oven for 1 hour.

3 egg whites
175g (6 oz) caster sugar
150ml (7 fl oz) double cream
1 × 200g tub Greek yoghurt

6 tablespoons lemon curd (see page 222), plus extra for drizzling
225g (8 oz) raspberries

Preheat the oven to 140°C/Fan 120°C/Gas 1. Line a baking sheet with baking parchment.

**1** Measure the egg whites into a large bowl (or the bowl of a free-standing machine). Whisk on high speed until white and fluffy, like a cloud. Still whisking on maximum speed, gradually add the sugar, a teaspoon at a time, until incorporated and the meringue is stiff and shiny and stands upright on the whisk.

**2** Spread the meringue mix over the lined baking sheet in an even layer. Cook in the preheated oven until crisp – this should take about 40–50 minutes.

**3** Remove from the paper on to a cooling rack and set aside until stone cold.

**4** In another bowl, whip the cream until thickened, but not stiff. Fold in the Greek yoghurt and then swirl the lemon curd into this cream and yoghurt mixture to give a marbled effect.

**5** Break the cooled meringue into bite-sized pieces and place in a large bowl with the lemon cream and the raspberries. Fold together gently and serve immediately in individual bowls with a final drizzle of lemon curd.

# Homemade Lemon Curd

A wonderful way of using up egg yolks, having made meringues.

COOK NOW
EAT LATER

**TO PREPARE AHEAD**
Keep in the fridge
for up to 3 months.

**TO FREEZE**
Not suitable.

**TO COOK IN THE AGA**
Cook in the Simmering
Oven for about 40
minutes, stirring
occasionally.

100g (4 oz) butter
225g (8 oz) caster sugar
5 egg yolks or 3 beaten eggs

grated zest and juice
of 3 lemons

**1** Measure the butter and sugar into a bowl. Stand this over a pan of simmering water and stir occasionally until the butter has melted.

**2** Stir the egg yolks (or eggs) and the lemon zest and juice into the butter mixture. Cook for about 25 minutes until the curd thickens, stirring occasionally. Do not allow to get too hot.

**3** Remove from the heat and pour into warm, clean jars.

# Lavender Crème Caramel

Make this classic with a twist the day before and turn out when serving, or the caramel will lose its colour. And, if you turn the caramel custard out too soon, the caramel stays in the bottom of the dish. This recipe also makes 6 small ramekins – reduce the cooking time to 20–30 minutes if you decide to do this.

butter for greasing
4 eggs
25g (1 oz) caster sugar
600ml (1 pint) milk
3–4 tablespoons fresh
   lavender leaves (pull
   off the stalk) or flowers

**Caramel**
100g (4 oz) granulated sugar
4 tablespoons water

**COOK NOW EAT LATER**

**TO PREPARE AHEAD**
Make the day before and keep in the fridge. Turn out just before serving.

**TO FREEZE**
Not suitable.

**TIP**
To make a caramel without the sugar crystallising, you must use a pan of stainless-steel, aluminium, enamel or copper. Never use a non-stick pan, which always seems to crystallise the sugar (and if it's got a dark lining, you can't see what is happening). Be careful not to let the caramel get too dark, or it will be bitter.

Preheat the oven to 150°C/Fan 130°C/Gas 2. Warm a 1.1 litre (2 pint) straight-sided round dish (a small soufflé dish is ideal) in the oven.

**1** First make the caramel. Measure the granulated sugar and water into a clean stainless steel pan. Dissolve the sugar slowly, stirring with a wooden spoon. When there are no sugar granules left, stop stirring and boil for a few minutes until the sugar turns a golden straw colour. Remove from the heat and pour quickly into the base of the warmed dish. Leave until cool then butter around the sides above the level of the caramel.

**2** Whisk the eggs with the caster sugar in a bowl until well mixed.

**3** Pour the milk into a saucepan with the lavender leaves or flowers and gently heat until you can still just dip your finger in for a moment, then strain through muslin on to the egg mixture. Stir and pour into the buttered dish.

*Recipe continued overleaf*

## TO COOK IN THE AGA

To make the caramel, dissolve the sugar and water in a pan on the Simmering Plate, stirring all the time until the sugar has dissolved. Take the spoon out of the pan and transfer the pan to the Boiling Plate. Boil rapidly until a golden straw colour. Finish steps 1 to 3. To cook the custard, place the soufflé dish in a small roasting tin lined with kitchen paper. Half fill with boiling water and carefully transfer to the third set of runners in the Roasting Oven for about 12–15 minutes until the custard is just set, but still has a wobble. Carefully transfer to the Simmering Oven for a further 45–60 minutes, or until set.

*Recipe continued*

**4** Stand the dish in a small roasting tin and fill the tin halfway with boiling water. Cook in the oven for 40–50 minutes or until the custard has set. Do not overcook the custard – check around the edge of the dish to make sure no bubbles are appearing.

**5** When cool, put into the fridge overnight so that the caramel is absorbed into the custard.

**6** To serve, place a plate (with a lip, as the caramel will spread) on top of the dish and turn upside down. Serve with pouring cream.

# Five-fruit Salad

This is a lovely fresh fruit salad. Do not add any sugar, just enjoy the natural sweetness from the fruit juices. I often serve this if the main pudding is very rich. If any is left, the fruits are delicious for breakfast.

**COOK NOW EAT LATER**

1 melon
2 mangoes
1 pink grapefruit

1 papaya (paw-paw)
225g (8 oz) raspberries

**TO PREPARE AHEAD**
The bulk of the salad can be made the day before. Just add the raspberries at the last minute.

**TO FREEZE**
Not suitable.

**1** First prepare the melon. Using a sharp knife, cut into quarters and remove the seeds. Remove the skin by slipping the knife between the flesh and the skin, then chop into large pieces.

**2** Peel the mangoes. Cut a thick slice from either side of the stone, then chop the flesh into large cubes.

**3** Using a knife with a serrated edge, peel and segment the grapefruit, saving any juice.

**4** Peel the papaya, take out the seeds with a teaspoon, and cut the flesh into pieces.

**5** Put all the prepared fruit, except for the raspberries, in a bowl, cover with clingfilm and put in the fridge, mixing from time to time.

**6** Just before serving, add the fresh raspberries and serve with crème fraîche if liked.

# White Chocolate Mousses

Really fast to make and memorable to eat.

40g (1½ oz) plain chocolate
(39 per cent cocoa solids)
75g (3 oz) Hobnob biscuits
(without chocolate coating),
coarsely crushed
225g (8 oz) strawberries,
thinly sliced
fresh mint sprigs to garnish

**White Chocolate Mousse**
1 × 200g bar 100% Belgium
white chocolate, broken
into small pieces
1 × 200g tub full-fat
cream cheese
200ml (7 fl oz) full-fat
crème fraîche

COOK NOW
EAT LATER

**TO PREPARE AHEAD**
Make up to 12 hours
ahead, cover and
keep in their rings
in the fridge.

**TO FREEZE**
Not suitable.

**TO COOK IN THE AGA**
Melt the chocolates
in separate bowls on
a tea-towel at the back
of the Aga several
hours ahead.

**TIP**
If you haven't any
metal rings, use small
empty chopped tomato
or baked bean cans.
Take off the top and
base with a can opener
and wash thoroughly.

You will need 6 × 7cm (2¾ in) metal rings. Place
on a baking sheet lined with non-stick baking paper.

**1** Break the plain chocolate into a medium-sized bowl
and melt over a pan of gently simmering water. Do not
allow the chocolate to become too hot. Add the biscuits
to the warm melted chocolate, stir to mix, then using
the back of a metal spoon press into the bottom of the
metal rings. Allow to set in the fridge.

**2** For the mousse, break the white chocolate into a bowl
and carefully melt over a pan of hot water. (Do not allow
the chocolate to get too hot or it will become grainy;
it should be slightly hotter than lukewarm.) Stir until
smooth. Set aside to cool a little to firm up. Add the cream
cheese and the crème fraîche, mixing until smooth.

**3** Neatly arrange the strawberry slices up the sides of the
rings and spoon the mousse mixture on to the individual
biscuit bases. Gently level the tops. Chill until firm.

**4** Transfer each mousse to a plate, remove the rings
and decorate with mint.

# Lemon Balm Ice Cream

A fresh ice cream for hot summer days. If you are unable to get lemon balm, use ginger mint or fresh mint, or leave the herb out – it will still be lovely! Using this recipe you do not need an ice cream maker or to re-whisk – it is just one process.

**COOK NOW EAT LATER**

**TO PREPARE AHEAD**
Prepare and freeze
for up to 1 month.

4 eggs, separated
finely grated zest and juice
    of 2 lemons
2 generous tablespoons lemon
    curd (see page 222)
2 tablespoons finely chopped
    fresh lemon balm
300ml (½ pint) pouring
    double cream
100g (4 oz) caster sugar

**To Serve**
fresh raspberries
    or raspberry coulis
fresh lemon balm leaves

**1** Whisk the egg yolks with the lemon zest and juice until well blended, then add the lemon curd and lemon balm.(This mixture is not very thick, don't worry.)

**2** In a separate bowl, whisk the cream until it forms soft peaks. Fold the egg yolks and lemon mixture into the cream.

**3** In a clean bowl, whisk the egg whites until stiff and gradually add the sugar, 1 teaspoon at a time, whisking continuously to form a stiff, shiny meringue mixture.

**4** Gently fold the lemon cream into the egg white meringue mixture. Turn the ice cream into a 1.4 litre (2½ pint) freezer container, cover, label and freeze overnight.

**5** Serve in scoopfuls with fresh raspberries or raspberry coulis, decorated with more lemon balm.

# Melon Sorbet

For a special occasion, use an orange-fleshed Cantaloupe or Charentais melon.
They are expensive but have a wonderful flavour and colour.

1 large Ogen or Galia melon
5 tablespoons of water
225g (8 oz) granulated sugar

pared rind and juice
of 1 lemon
300ml (½ pint) water

**COOK NOW EAT LATER**

**TO PREPARE AHEAD**
Prepare and freeze
for up to 1 month.

**1** Cut the melon into quarters. Remove the skin and
seeds and process the flesh until smooth.

**2** Measure the 5 tablespoons of water, the sugar and
the lemon rind into a medium heavy-based saucepan.
Dissolve slowly over a gentle heat. When the sugar has
completely dissolved, boil rapidly until the syrup is tacky
and a short thread can be formed if the syrup is pulled
between 2 teaspoons. Carefully remove and discard the
lemon rind.

**3** Mix the warm syrup together with the melon purée,
lemon juice and the 300ml (½ pint) water. Allow to cool.

**4** Freeze the mixture overnight or until icy, then whisk
until smooth and return to the freezer. (Or use an ice
cream machine if you have one, following the
manufacturer's instructions.)

**5** Serve in well-chilled goblets.

# Orange Curd Ice Cream
## with Passionfruit and Orange

There are some delicious flavours here. When buying ready-made curds, check the labels to see that the contents are just butter, sugar and eggs, and no E numbers.

**COOK NOW EAT LATER**

**TO PREPARE AHEAD**
Prepare and freeze the ice cream for up to 1 month. Prepare the oranges and passionfruit, cover and keep in the fridge for up to 24 hours. Remove the ice cream from the freezer 5–10 minutes before serving.

4 eggs, separated
100g (4 oz) caster sugar
300ml (½ pint) double cream, lightly whipped
finely grated zest of 1 medium orange

6 tablespoons luxury orange curd
1–1½ oranges per person
¼ passionfruit per person
fresh mint leaves to decorate

**1** Place the egg yolks in a small bowl and whisk until well blended.

**2** In a clean bowl, whisk the egg whites until stiff using an electric hand whisk, then whisk in the sugar 1 teaspoon at a time until stiff and glossy.

**3** Fold the cream into the egg yolks, with the orange zest and curd. Mix in 1 spoonful of egg white and carefully fold in the remaining egg white.

**4** Turn the ice cream into a 1.4 litre (2½ pint) plastic container, cover and freeze overnight.

**5** Segment the oranges. Cut each passionfruit in half, and scoop out the pulp. Mix together.

**6** Serve the tangy fruit mixture with the orange curd ice cream, and decorate with mint.

COOK NOW, EAT LATER

✴

# Home
# Baking

## CHAPTER NINE

As you know, home baking is one of my passions, and I love creating new cakes, biscuits and traybakes. One of the principal advantages of home baking is that most cakes can be frozen: you can cool them, wrap them well and freeze as soon as possible after baking, and they will emerge as good as new after a couple of months. Cakes might need icing after defrosting (many icings look best when fresh), and scones and muffins will need to be oven-refreshed, but the basic work has all been done well in advance.

Baking needs to be a little more precise than many other aspects of cookery. For instance, it really is essential to weigh everything correctly. Usually people weigh 'heavy', so you should check your scales against a packet of sugar or butter. The right size of tin is essential as well: have a ruler or tape measure handy to check the width and depth of each tin. So often people say a particular sponge recipe hasn't worked, and it's turned out that they've used the wrong tin. It makes a huge difference.

And ingredients are very important too. Use natural sugars if you can, as they contain no dyes. All the recipes call for large eggs, and organic are best. Be careful with baking powder: if you use even fractionally too much, the cake will rise up then fall down again! Fats are a contentious issue now. The method I use for mixing cakes before baking is the all-in-one method. All the ingredients are put into the bowl then beaten together with a hand whisk until smooth. I once used baking margarines with an 80 per cent fat content, and these, like butter, would be slightly softened before mixing. However, these margarines are no longer available so I use a 'spread for baking' instead, such as Stork Tub, Flora Original or Flora Buttery. Because of the reduced fat content, these need to be used straight from the fridge, otherwise they would be too soft and the cake mix would be too runny. Always look at the packaging: ideally you want over 60 per cent fat margarine, to use at room temperature.

# Fresh Raspberry Scones

Fresh blueberries can replace the raspberries if wished, but we prefer the raspberries!
The scone dough is very deep to cut out once layered with the raspberries, so flour the
cutter well between each cutting to prevent the dough sticking. The large scone made
from the trimmings is perfect sliced for the family.

450g (1 lb) self-raising flour
4 teaspoons baking powder
100g (4 oz) butter, softened
50g (2 oz) caster sugar

2 eggs
milk
about 100g (4 oz)
   fresh raspberries

Lightly grease two baking trays. Preheat the oven
to 220°C/Fan 200°C/Gas 7.

**1** Measure the flour and baking powder into a large bowl.
Add the butter and rub in with the fingertips until the
mixture resembles fine breadcrumbs. Stir in the sugar.

**2** Break the eggs into a measuring jug, then make up to
300ml (½ pint) with milk. Stir the egg and milk mixture
into the flour – you may not need it all – and mix to a soft
but not sticky dough.

**3** Turn out on to a lightly floured work surface, knead
lightly and then roll out to a rectangle about 2cm (¾ in)
thick. Cut the rectangle of dough into 2 equal pieces.

**4** Scatter the fresh raspberries evenly over 1 piece of
dough. Top with the second rectangle of dough. Cut
into as many rounds as possible with a fluted 5cm (2 in)
cutter, and place them on the prepared baking trays.
Gently push the trimmings together to form 1 large
scone, and score the top with a sharp knife. Brush the
tops of the scones with a little extra milk, or any egg
and milk left in the jug.

**5** Bake in the preheated oven for about 15 minutes or
until the scones are well risen and a pale golden brown.
(The large scone will need about a further 5 minutes.)
Lift on to a wire rack to cool. Eat as fresh as possible.

### TO PREPARE AHEAD
Best eaten on the day
of making. If you must,
store the cooked scones
in the fridge for 1 day.
To serve, refresh in
a preheated oven at
180°C/Fan 160°C/Gas
4 for about 10 minutes.

### TO FREEZE
These freeze extremely
well. Freeze the cooled
scones in plastic bags
for up to 6 months.
Thaw in the plastic
bags for 2–3 hours at
room temperature, and
reheat as above to serve.

### TO COOK IN THE AGA
Cook on the grid shelf
on the lowest set of
runners of the
Roasting Oven for
about 10–15 minutes.

# Herb and Parmesan Soft Rolls

This is a quick and easy way of making rolls. You can make them by hand or use a dough hook which will save time and effort. This recipe can also be used to make two small 450g (1 lb) loaves, but naturally they will take a little longer to bake.

**COOK NOW EAT LATER**

### TO PREPARE AHEAD

Complete step 1 the day before. Or the rolls can be baked the day before they are needed and then refreshed in a moderate oven at 180°C/Fan 160°C/Gas 4 for 15 minutes when required.

### TO FREEZE

Cool the cooked rolls completely, pack into a plastic bag and freeze for up to 3 months. Thaw at room temperature. Refresh in a moderate oven as above for about 10–15 minutes.

500g (1 lb 2 oz) strong white flour, plus extra for kneading
4 tablespoons olive oil, plus extra for glazing
350ml (12 fl oz) warm water
3 teaspoons salt
1 × 7g packet fast-action yeast
50g (2 oz) Parmesan or Parmesan-style hard cheese, freshly grated, plus extra for sprinkling

25g (1 oz) fresh chives, snipped
a good handful of fresh basil leaves, chopped
a good handful of fresh parsley, chopped
sunflower seeds

**1** Measure the flour, oil, water, salt and yeast into the mixer and mix using the dough hook for 5–8 minutes – the mixture will look quite wet – or mix by hand. Put into a large oiled bowl and cover with clingfilm. Place in the fridge overnight.

**2** The next day take the dough out of the fridge. It should have doubled in size. Leave the dough on one side for 1 hour to bring back to room temperature, then knock back by kneading in the mixer or on a floured surface for 5 minutes by hand.

**3** Add the cheese and herbs and continue to knead until they are well incorporated.

**4** Divide the dough into 20 pieces and roll into balls. Place these close together on a greased baking sheet, and cover with an oiled plastic bag. (A dry cleaners' suit plastic bag is ideal – just tie a knot in the plastic where the hanger hole is.) Leave to prove in a warm place for about 30 minutes, or until the rolls have doubled in size.

Meanwhile, preheat the oven to 200°C/Fan 180°C/Gas 6.

**5** Lightly glaze the rolls with oil and sprinkle with sunflower seeds and Parmesan.

**6** Bake in the preheated oven for about 20–25 minutes until well risen, golden and the rolls sound hollow when tapped on the base. Best served warm.

### TO COOK IN THE AGA

Bake the rolls for about 20–30 minutes on the grid shelf on the floor of the Roasting Oven. Check after 15 minutes. Remove the grid shelf and put the baking sheet directly on the floor of the Roasting Oven to brown the bases.

# Peppadew and Cheddar Scone Bake

Lovely for a lunch box or with soup or salad. Serve with butter or cream cheese. These can be cut into more than 12 pieces if you want a smaller slice.

**COOK NOW EAT LATER**

## TO PREPARE AHEAD

Bake up to 24 hours in advance. Reheat and refresh in the tin in a moderate oven at 180°C/Fan 160°C/Gas 4 for about 10 minutes.

## TO FREEZE

Allow the baked scone to cool completely, then pack into a strong polythene bag and freeze for up to 3 months. Thaw at room temperature and reheat and refresh in a moderate oven as above to serve.

## TO COOK IN THE AGA

Slide the traybake tin on to the grid shelf on the floor of the Roasting Oven for about 15 minutes or until a perfect golden brown. Slide the plain cold sheet on to the second set of runners and bake for a further 5–10 minutes until firm.

450g (1 lb) self-raising flour
4 teaspoons baking powder
1 teaspoon salt
½ teaspoon mustard powder
freshly ground black pepper
100g (4 oz) butter, at room temperature

225g (8 oz) mature Cheddar, grated
100g (4 oz) peppadew bell peppers, drained and finely sliced
2 eggs
milk

Lightly grease a 30 × 23cm (12 × 9 in) traybake tin or roasting tin. Preheat the oven to 220°C/Fan 200°C/Gas 7.

**1** Measure the flour, baking powder, salt and mustard powder into a large bowl and add a little black pepper. Add the butter and rub into the flour using the fingertips until the mixture resembles fine breadcrumbs. Stir in the cheese and peppers.

**2** Break the eggs into a measuring jug, beat together, and make up to 300ml (½ pint) with milk. Add to the flour mixture, mixing to form a soft dough.

**3** Knead the dough quickly and lightly until smooth, then roll out on a lightly floured work surface to an oblong to fit the roasting tin. Mark into 12 squares and brush the top with a little milk.

**4** Bake in the preheated oven for about 20 minutes until the scone is well risen and golden. Turn out on to a wire rack to cool. Break apart to serve.

# Apple and Lemon Drop Scones

Drop scones and Scotch pancakes are the same thing. It's essential to make them and eat them straightaway while still warm, with butter or lemon curd.

100g (4 oz) plain flour
1½ teaspoons baking powder
25g (1 oz) caster sugar
finely grated zest of 1 lemon,
   plus 1 teaspoon lemon juice
25g (1 oz) butter, melted

1 egg
100ml (4 fl oz) milk
1 small Cox's apple, peeled
vegetable oil for greasing

**1** Measure the flour, baking powder, sugar and lemon zest into a bowl and mix lightly. Make a well in the centre then mix in the butter, egg, milk and lemon juice. Gradually draw the dry ingredients into the liquid to make a smooth thick batter. Coarsely grate in the apple.

**2** Prepare a griddle or heavy-based frying pan (preferably non-stick) by heating and greasing with oil or white vegetable fat.

**3** Drop the mixture in spoonfuls on to the hot griddle, spacing the mixture well apart. When bubbles rise to the surface, turn the scones over with a palette knife and cook them on the other side for a further 30 seconds to 1 minute until they are golden brown.

**4** Lift off on to a wire rack and cover them with a clean tea-towel to keep them soft. Continue cooking until all of the mixture has been used. Serve warm.

### TO PREPARE AHEAD
The batter can be made the day before, but grate in the apple at the last minute. Best freshly made to order.

### TO FREEZE
Not suitable as they go rather rubbery.

### TO COOK ON THE AGA
Grease the Simmering Plate lightly with a little oil (use a pad of kitchen paper to do this). If your Simmering Plate is particularly hot, it may be necessary to lift the lid for a couple of minutes to reduce the heat slightly. Spoon the mixture on to the plate in tablespoons, spacing them well apart (about 4 at a time). When bubbles rise to the surface, turn the drop scones over with a palette knife, and cook on the other side for a further 30 seconds or until golden brown. Lift off and serve.

# Ginger and Orange Cake
## with Mascarpone Icing

A delicious and light cake, best kept in the fridge because of the icing.
This cake is a true favourite with all who work with me!

**COOK NOW EAT LATER**

### TO PREPARE AHEAD

Make the cakes and store in an airtight container for up to 3 days before filling and icing. Make the filling/icing when you need it.

### TO FREEZE

The cakes freeze well un-iced. Wrap and freeze for up to 3 months. Thaw for about 4 hours at room temperature, then fill and ice.

### TO COOK IN THE AGA

Bake on the grid shelf on the floor of the Roasting Oven with the cold shelf on the second set of runners for about 25 minutes. Turn halfway through baking.

275g (10 oz) self-raising flour
1 level teaspoon baking powder
225g (8 oz) baking margarine or butter, at room temperature
225g (8 oz) caster sugar
4 eggs
finely grated zest of 1 orange
5–6 bulbs stem ginger in syrup, coarsely chopped, plus syrup
1 × 250g tub mascarpone cheese

Preheat the oven to 180°C/Fan 160°C/Gas 4. Base-line 2 × 20cm (8 in) deep sandwich tins with non-stick paper, and grease well.

**1** Measure the flour, baking powder, margarine or butter, sugar, eggs and the grated orange zest into a large mixing bowl. Rinse the syrup from 3–4 bulbs of the ginger and then add them to the mixing bowl (this will prevent the ginger from sinking). Using an electric hand mixer, mix well until thoroughly blended. Divide the mixture evenly between the prepared tins and level out.

**2** Bake in the centre of the preheated oven for 20–25 minutes until golden brown and shrinking away from the sides of the tin. Leave to cool for a few moments then turn out.

**3** For the filling/icing, beat the mascarpone with 2 tablespoons of the ginger syrup. When the cakes are completely cold, sandwich together with half of this mixture. Spread the remainder on top of the cake and sprinkle over the remaining coarsely chopped ginger.

# Double Chocolate Chip Brownie Cake

A quick and easy chocolate cake. Making two loaves
allows you to freeze one for another day.

**COOK NOW
EAT LATER**

### TO PREPARE AHEAD
Bake and ice up to 3 days
ahead. (The icing is
better made nearer the
time of serving, though.)

### TO FREEZE
Cool, pack and freeze
the un-iced cakes for
up to 3 months. Thaw
at room temperature
for about 4 hours
before icing.

### TO COOK IN THE AGA
Place the tins on the
grill rack in a large
roasting tin. Slide on to
the lowest set of runners
in the Roasting Oven
with the cold sheet
on the second set of
runners. Bake for about
30 minutes until the
cakes are well risen and
set. Carefully transfer
to the Simmering Oven
for about 25 minutes.
For the icing, melt the
chocolate and butter
in the Simmering Oven
for about 10 minutes.

100g (4 oz) ground almonds
225g (8 oz) baking margarine
   or butter, at room
   temperature
175g (6 oz) self-raising flour
225g (8 oz) light muscovado
   sugar
50g (2 oz) cocoa powder
5 eggs
2 level teaspoons baking
   powder
150g (5 oz) white chocolate
   buttons

**Icing**
200g (7 oz) dark chocolate
   (Bournville)
50g (2 oz) butter
25g (1 oz) white chocolate
   buttons

Grease and line 2 × 450g (1 lb) loaf tins (top measurement
17 × 11cm/6½ × 4 in). Preheat the oven to 180°C/Fan
160°C/Gas 4.

**1** Measure all the ingredients for the cake, except the
white buttons, into a bowl and mix until smooth. Fold
in the white chocolate buttons and pour into the tins.
Level the surface.

**2** Bake in the middle of the preheated oven for about
1 hour or until well risen, firm to the touch and shrinking
away from the sides of the tin. Allow the cakes to cool
on a wire rack.

**3** For the icing, put the dark chocolate and butter into
a bowl. Place over a pan of simmering water to melt.
Stir, leave for 2 minutes, then spread over the top of
the cakes. Dot the white chocolate buttons on to the
warm chocolate icing.

# Lemon and Lime Traybake

For a special occasion, or if the limes are a reasonable price, you could use the juice and zest of 6 limes for a really fresh taste, omitting the lemon.

275g (10 oz) self-raising flour
225g (8 oz) caster sugar
4 eggs
225g (8 oz) baking margarine
  or butter, at room
  temperature
2 teaspoons baking powder

finely grated zest of 2 lemons
finely grated zest of 2 limes
2 tablespoons milk

**Topping**
175g (6 oz) granulated sugar
juice of 2 limes and 1 lemon

COOK NOW EAT LATER

Line a 30 × 23cm (12 × 9 in) traybake tin with baking parchment and grease well. Preheat the oven to 180°C/ Fan 160°C/Gas 4.

**1** Measure all of the cake ingredients into a large bowl and mix well, using an electric beater.

**2** Spoon into the prepared tin and gently level the top.

**3** Bake in the preheated oven for 30–35 minutes or until well risen and pale golden brown.

**4** Mix together the sugar and lime and lemon juices for the topping and pour over the warm cake. Allow to cool before cutting into squares.

**TO PREPARE AHEAD**
Bake and complete the cake and store, iced or un-iced, in an airtight container for 2–3 days.

**TO FREEZE**
Leave whole. Pack and freeze, iced or un-iced, for up to 2 months. Thaw at room temperature for 2–3 hours. Cut into squares to serve.

**TO COOK IN THE AGA**
Bake on the lowest set of runners in the Roasting Oven and slide the cold sheet on the second set of runners. Bake for about 30–35 minutes until pale golden brown and shrinking away from the sides of the tin.

# Banoffee Traybake

A variation on a traybake, with a naughty toffee icing.
Best eaten at room temperature.

**COOK NOW
EAT LATER**

### TO PREPARE AHEAD
Store the iced cake in
an airtight container
for 2–3 days.

### TO FREEZE
Leave whole. If freezing
the cake iced, open-
freeze first then wrap
and freeze for up to
2 months. Or freeze
the un-iced cake.
Unwrap and thaw for
about 4 hours at room
temperature.

### TO COOK IN THE AGA
Bake on the lowest
set of runners in the
Roasting Oven and
slide the cold sheet
on to the second set of
runners. Bake for about
30–35 minutes until
pale golden brown and
shrinking away from
the sides of the tin.

175g (6 oz) baking margarine
or butter, at room
temperature
250g (9 oz) caster sugar
3 eggs, beaten
3 ripe bananas, mashed
350g (12 oz) self-raising flour
2 teaspoons baking powder
3 tablespoons milk

**Toffee Topping**
50g (2 oz) butter
50g (2 oz) light muscovado
sugar
1 × 397g can sweetened
condensed milk

Line a 30 × 23cm (12 × 9 in) traybake tin or roasting tin
with foil and grease well. Preheat the oven to 180°C/Fan
160°C/Gas 4.

**1** Measure all the cake ingredients into a large mixing
bowl and, using an electric beater, mix until smooth.
Spoon into the lined tin and gently level the top. Bake
in the oven for about 40–45 minutes or until well risen
and golden. Cool in the tin.

**2** For the topping, measure the butter, sugar and
condensed milk into a saucepan and heat gently until
the sugar has dissolved. Bring up to the boil stirring
continuously, and simmer for a few minutes until
smooth and starting to thicken.

**3** Take off the heat and cool slightly, then pour over the
cool cake. Spread out evenly with a small palette knife.
Allow the caramel to set on the cake before cutting
the traybake into squares with a hot knife.

# Sultana Spice Traybake

This recipe is egg free, therefore the texture is not as light as that of some traybakes and it is quite a thick mixture when it goes into the tin. It is fairly plain so is ideal to have for elevenses.

COOK NOW
EAT LATER

**TO PREPARE AHEAD**
This can be made a couple of days in advance, but is best eaten as fresh as possible.

**TO FREEZE**
Bake the traybake and cool. Wrap and freeze for up to 3 months. Thaw at room temperature for about 3–4 hours.

**TO COOK IN THE AGA**
Bake on the grid shelf on the floor of the Roasting Oven with the cold sheet on the second set of runners for about 20–25 minutes until golden brown and firm to the touch.

500g (1 lb 2 oz) self-raising flour
275g (10 oz) baking margarine or butter, at room temperature
2 level teaspoons baking powder
1 teaspoon mixed spice
175g (6 oz) caster sugar
175g (6 oz) sultanas
grated zest of 1 orange
300ml (½ pint) milk
demerara sugar

Base-line a 30 × 23cm (12 × 9 in) traybake tin or roasting tin with greased baking paper. Preheat the oven to 200°C/Fan 180°C/Gas 6.

**1** Measure all the ingredients, except the milk and demerara sugar, into a bowl and mix with an electric hand whisk, or by hand, until evenly blended.

**2** Gradually add the milk, stirring all the time, until well incorporated.

**3** Spoon into the lined tin and level out, then sprinkle generously with demerara sugar.

**4** Bake in the preheated oven for about 30–35 minutes until golden brown and firm to the touch. Allow to cool in the tin before turning out.

# Chocolate and Rum Cake

A very moist cake. This recipe was used for the chocolate cake competition
at our local village show. I was the judge and thought it was delicious.
All 12 entries were beautiful, which means it is a sound simple recipe.
I've added some rum to the icing, but you could add brandy instead.

50g (2 oz) cocoa powder
200ml (7 fl oz) boiling water
175g (6 oz) self-raising flour
1 rounded teaspoon
    baking powder
100g (4 oz) butter, softened
275g (10 oz) caster sugar
2 eggs

**Icing**
100g (4 oz) butter, softened
225g (8 oz) icing sugar
2 dessertspoons cocoa powder
2 tablespoons rum or brandy
    (or water)

COOK NOW
EAT LATER

Grease and base-line 2 × 20cm (8 in) deep sandwich
tins. Preheat the oven to 180°C/Fan 160°C/Gas 4.

**1** In a large bowl whisk the cocoa powder with the
boiling water, adding it slowly at first, until a smooth
consistency. Add the remaining ingredients and blend
together using an electric hand whisk.

**2** Divide the mixture between the tins and bake in the
middle of the oven for about 30–35 minutes, or until
the cakes start to shrink away from the sides of the
tins. Loosen from the tins and cool on a wire rack.

**3** For the icing, beat the soft butter until very soft, then
add the icing sugar and cocoa powder with the rum,
brandy or water. Mix until smooth then sandwich the
cakes together with one-third of the icing. Use the
remaining icing to cover the top and sides of the cake.

### TO PREPARE AHEAD
Store the completed
iced cake in an
airtight container
for up to a week.

### TO FREEZE
Freeze the completed
iced cake in a round
plastic freezer
container for up to
1 month. Thaw for
about 4 hours at
room temperature.

### TO COOK IN THE AGA
Slide the tins on to
the grid shelf on the
floor of the Roasting
Oven with the cold
sheet on the second
set of runners for
about 20–25 minutes,
turning once halfway
through, until the
cakes are shrinking
away from the sides
of the tins.

# Orange Chocolate Shortbread Biscuits

*A variation on an old classic and very easy to make.*
*The chocolate becomes crisp and crunchy.*

**COOK NOW
EAT LATER**

**TO PREPARE AHEAD**
Bake, cool and store
the biscuits in an
airtight container
for up to 1 week.

**TO FREEZE**
Pack the cooked and
cooled biscuits into a
freezer-proof container
and freeze for up to
2 months. Thaw at
room temperature
for 1–2 hours.

**TO COOK IN THE AGA**
Place the baking
sheet on the floor of
the Roasting Oven for
4 minutes. Take out of
the oven, put the grid
shelf on the floor and
return the biscuits
to the grid shelf. Cook
for a further 4 minutes
until just pale golden
at the edges. Transfer
to the Simmering
Oven for a further
30–35 minutes until
the biscuits are
cooked through.

175g (6 oz) butter, softened
75g (3 oz) caster sugar
175g (6 oz) plain flour
75g (3 oz) cornflour
   or semolina

100g (4 oz) orange milk
   chocolate, chopped into
   small pieces

Lightly grease two baking trays. Preheat the oven
to 190°C/Fan 170°C/Gas 5.

**1** Measure the butter and sugar into a food processor
and process until soft. Add the flour and cornflour or
semolina and process until beginning to form coarse
breadcrumbs. Scrape down the sides, remove the blade
and stir in the chocolate pieces.

**2** Shape the mixture into 20 even-sized balls and put
on to the prepared baking trays. Flatten each ball
with a fork.

**3** Bake in the preheated oven for about 15–20 minutes
until the edges of the biscuits are golden. Allow to cool
for a few minutes then transfer to a wire rack until cold.

# Mega Chocolate Cookies

For speed you can use chocolate chips, but we like the large chunks of roughly chopped chocolate! Of course you can make normal-sized biscuits from the same mixture.

**COOK NOW
EAT LATER**

## TO PREPARE AHEAD

Make up to 2 days ahead, store in an airtight container and refresh in a moderate oven at 180°C/Fan 160°C/Gas 4 for 8–10 minutes. Cool to let them become crisp, and serve.

## TO FREEZE

Cook and cool the cookies completely. Pack and freeze for up to 2 months. Thaw at room temperature for 1–2 hours. Refresh in a warm oven as above.

## TO COOK IN THE AGA

Cook on the grid shelf on the floor of the Roasting Oven with the cold shelf on the second set of runners for about 15–20 minutes, turning round after about 10 minutes. In the Aga the cookies will spread slightly more than in a conventional oven.

225g (8 oz) butter, softened
175g (6 oz) caster sugar
100g (4 oz) light muscovado
    sugar
1 teaspoon vanilla extract

2 eggs, beaten
300g (11 oz) self-raising flour
225g (8 oz) plain chocolate,
    cut into chunky pieces

Lightly grease four baking trays. Preheat the oven to 190°C/Fan 170°C/Gas 5.

**1** Measure the butter and sugars into a large bowl and mix thoroughly until evenly blended. Add the vanilla extract to the eggs, then add these gradually to the mixture in the bowl, beating well between each addition. Next add the flour, mix in and lastly stir in the chocolate chunks.

**2** Spoon large tablespoons of the mixture on to the prepared baking trays, leaving room for the cookies to spread.(You will only be able to fit about 4 per tray!)

**3** Bake in the top of the oven for about 15 minutes or until the cookies are just golden. Allow the cookies to cool on the tray for a couple of minutes before lifting off with a palette knife or fish slice. Allow to cool completely on a wire rack.

# Apricot and Walnut Breakfast Muffins

Don't expect these to be very sweet: they are more like traditional American muffins. They're perfect for breakfast served warm, and are delicious with honey.

275g (10 oz) self-raising flour
1 level teaspoon baking powder
2 eggs
75g (3 oz) caster sugar
225ml (8 fl oz) milk
100g (4 oz) butter, melted
  and cooled slightly

1 teaspoon vanilla extract
175g (6 oz) ready-to-eat dried
  apricots, snipped into
  small pieces
50g (2 oz) shelled walnuts,
  roughly chopped

Arrange 12 paper muffin cases in a muffin tin if you have one, or on a baking sheet. Preheat the oven to 200°C/Fan 180°C/Gas 6.

**1** Measure all the ingredients into a bowl and beat well to mix. Divide the mixture between the paper muffin cases.

**2** Bake in the middle of the preheated oven for about 25–30 minutes or until well risen, cooked through and golden. Remove to a wire rack to cool.

COOK NOW
EAT LATER

### TO PREPARE AHEAD
Best eaten freshly made, but can be baked 2 days ahead and refreshed in a moderate oven at 180°C/Fan 160°C/Gas 4 for 10 minutes.

### TO FREEZE
Cool, pack and freeze for up to 4 months. Thaw at room temperature for about 2 hours. Refresh in the oven as above to serve.

### TO COOK ON THE AGA
Bake on the grid shelf on the floor of the Roasting Oven for about 10–15 minutes until golden brown and well risen, then slide the cold shelf on to the second set of runners for a further 10 minutes or until cooked through.

# INDEX

✦

## THE APP

For the first time, recipes from a selection of Mary Berry's books are also available in a new app. In Mary We Trust features over 50 of Mary's step-by-step recipes including Family Lasagne, Mexican Spicy Lamb, Orange and Honey Roast Chicken, Double Haddock and Herb Fishcakes, Beef Wellington, and Chargrilled Vegetable Strudel, plus show-stopping cakes and puddings. For the festive season there are also recipes for a traditional Christmas dinner, including Roast Turkey and all the trimmings.

Let Mary guide you through the planning, shopping and timings for meals with her shopping lists and unique multiple timer for iPad. Set the timer for up to three different dishes at a time and relax. Put your trust in Mary Berry.

# THANK YOUS

Knowing that most of us have very busy lives, I felt that the idea of preparing dishes ahead and keeping them in the fridge, or in some cases freezing them, would make life easier. They are then ready to cook on the day for family or when you have friends round – you can cook now and eat later.

We are a team here at Watercroft. Lucy Young, who has been part of our family for 24 years, is in charge, her standards fly high and together we will only accept the best results in the kitchen. Lucy is Jack of all trades – we sit down and plan the recipes using the finest quality ingredients, not too many in one recipe, and we are very particular to ensure they are foolproof. Lucy makes a master schedule and gradually, with the help of Lucinda McCord, we test the recipes here at home and bring the book together. Times have changed since we wrote the original book – we no longer use dried herbs as fresh herbs are so readily available and we use slightly less cream nowadays! – and there are always plenty of people to taste and comment on the results. The book evolves over the months before we reach the final design and jacket, which our publishers create with such expertise.

So now our thanks to our publishers Headline. Jonathan Taylor boldly commissioned us to update this book with new design and photos and more recipes, hints and tips. Jo Roberts-Miller a brilliant editor who didn't miss a trick and is a joy to work with. Muna Reyal who guided the book to deadline and Felicity Bryan our literary agent who is always at the end of the phone. Thanks also to Martin Poole for the stunning photography, Smith & Gilmour for their design, and Kim Morphew and her assistant Poppy Campbell as home economists.

I am so grateful to you all.